little ★ luna

poetry | prose | art

Alita L. A. Powell

little★luna
Copyright © 2020 by Alita L. A. Powell

Tellwell Talent
www.tellwell.ca

ISBN
978-0-2288-3364-2 (Paperback)
978-0-2288-3365-9 (eBook)

★ ACKNOWLEDGEMENTS ★

This book would not be in your hands, dear reader, without the combined hours of energy and support from so many people all around the world.

THANK YOU

First and foremost, to each and every one of the 44 unbelievably kind and talented illustrators, across the globe, who willingly and graciously gave these pages life. I cannot thank you all enough. Eternally grateful to have a piece of you, wonderful people, forever inked in these pages.

Hannah - for repeatedly reading my mind across continents and oceans. You are an artistic magician. I love you so, my Boshana, and owe you a lifetime supply of yam fries and mayo.

Jada - for your unconditional love and support in every form from the moment I was born. Life simply would not be what it is today without you, my beautiful, endlessly inspiring, sister.

Will - for helping me feel more than I ever could have imagined, and filling my life with love and laughter.

Mum - for every rhyming birthday card and Dr. Seuss story before bed when we were kids. And for taking the time to edit every one of these words and delivering your honest corrections and reactions. Love you!

Chris McNeill - my first poetic critic and favourite teacher who said he couldn't wait to read the book I'd one day write. You were right, Mr. McNeill. I hope somehow you're reading this from up there.

My Tellwell Team - for making this such a positive experience, from the first phone call. I am so grateful to Ejay, Gezel and all of the amazing Tellwell team who made this dream into a reality.

And, of course, thanks to YOU, dear
reader, for everything hereafter.

★ INTRODUCTION ★

In these pages you will find a piece of my heart and over 200 illustrations from wonderful artists all over the world. All pictures are drawn/painted/ collaged by myself, talented friends and family, or an international artist I've never had the pleasure of meeting, who kindly granted me permission to print their work alongside my words. Each piece of art was either requested specifically, inspired by the poem that the artist chose, or found serendipitously and inspired the words alongside it.

The collective amount of hours put into all of the artwork is a lifetime and I truly thank each of you with all of my heart. I could not have done this without every single one of you. Each artist is credited under their work (unless drawn by me).

★

The journey of this book began seven or eight years ago, as little sentences stuck in my head on repeat that I would have to jot down in notebooks or quickly type out in order to get them out of my mind. Last year, I randomly began reading through hundreds of pages and notepads and shabby ripped diaries filled throughout the years, and realised I had never shared any of my writing with anyone. So, to conquer my fear and as a boost to my mental health, I began an anonymous poetry page online under the name "littleluna" and put pieces up next to art I would find that inspired me or seemed to fit perfectly. I love poetry. And rhymes. And line art. I grew up falling asleep to the whimsical words of Dr. Seuss and later fell in love with the sophisticated rhyming rhythms of Shakespeare. The online poetry page made me realise that my words were connecting to others, in their own realities, and that with the amount of poems already produced, I could potentially put a book together.

I share that to begin with because: 1. I am an avid believer, and 2. this book - quite literally - all in perfect timing, fell into place:

The random desire to read through seven years of neglected notebooks and forgotten boxes of saved scrap papers.

Which inspired: The little★luna Instagram poetry page.

Which prompted: The complete spur-of-the-moment Google search for "Canadian self-publishing companies".

Immediately followed by: The Tellwell number dial and heartening 45-minute phone call with Ejay.

Kick starting: The next six months of piecing together this book. Which just so happened to start right before a worldwide pandemic, forcing everyone indoors for weeks on end, cancelling all months of pre-planned travel and returning all of said expenses into my bank account, which paid for the publishing package and all of the incredible art.

Little dominoes, each leading perfectly to the next. No step possible without the one prior.

The 200+ pages you're about to read are all dear to me. My hope is that within these pages you find **a piece of yourself** that inspires a smile, a tear, a question, new found compassion, colourful conversation, or perhaps an image you'll sketch out / paint/ write down. Simply put, to inspire and be inspired, in a continuous, wonderful circle.

WHY I LIKE POETRY

The beautiful thing about words is
they take on their true meaning
when we need them most.

No other time than when the words
fill and spill onto that page
have they arranged in the same
staged way in my mind.

Once out in the world, they're ready,
awaiting the perfect, inevitable timing
for someone to find their silver lining,
and mould their own meaning
to each sentence's syncopated syllables.

So read away. Take what you need today.

PARTED

I've packed my bags and parted ways
from hundreds of new smiling faces
and extravagant places that
I'll keep forever in memory.

What a great gift and often a torment it is
to see so much and meet so many
and always end the day by parting ways.

Art: Mikaela Kruse

ONE, TWO, TEA

Never underestimate the power of these three:

1. Music
2. The Sea
3. A cup of tea in good company

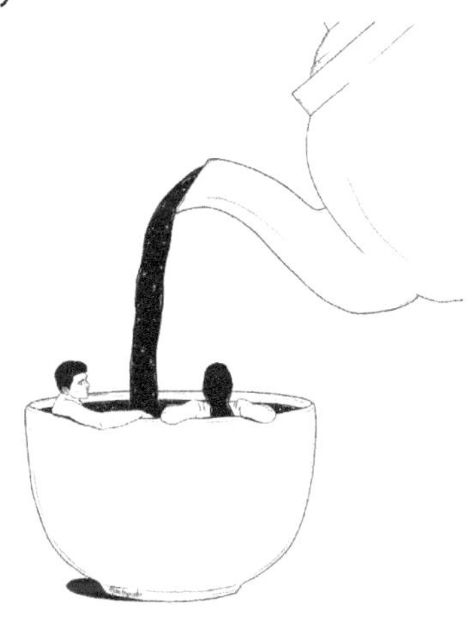

Art: @poetryncolor

ART/ CREATION

/ärt/ /krēˈāSH(ə)n/

Using your own unique,
untouched imagination,
introduces you to parts of yourself
that nothing else can access,
that no one else can simply,
compactly express,
in words that do justice
to who it is you become
and what it is you confess,
when you go into that mess
of unknown exploration.

Doubt leaves when you
roll up your sleeves,
and let the sweat breathe,
to share yourself with the world,
waiting in restless anticipation.

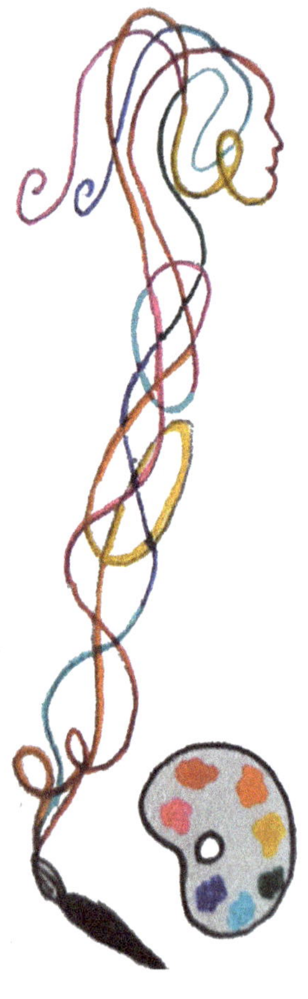

THE IDEA OF US

I think I'm in love   with the idea of us

being blessings for each other's broken hearts

and bleeding into each other's thoughts and whatnots.

Kneading, knitting, knotting our forgotten ways

into each other's maze of shifting, twisting

forget-me-

nots.

BY THE SEA

And
I replied,
"By the sea, please.
No particular place really,
just as long as I can see her
and she can see me."

DIMPLES

Forgive me if
my dimples' final count
falls short of
how far my gratitude goes
and grasps the shores
of every seaside mile I've spent
smiling and embracing a world
above and beyond
what I had ever guessed was in store.

STARDUST FINGERS

PART I

My stardust fingers
trace pathways over pale, moonlit skin
and try to remember a certain face.
My fingers linger over lost loving and
I recall a small, glimmering smile and
seashells humming their hymns.

I remember the ocean and you laughing.
I remember softened sea glass between our toes
and a faint fear of losing that moment
before I was ready. Steady. Rocking the boat.
We didn't paddle at the same pace.

I remember that.
The simple rhythm of us walking, rocking
back and forth, slowly forced out of sync,
sinking into a silent awkwardness.

I remember pieces of you.
But your face is still faint and the paint
won't stain my memory as well as I'd like.

PART II

I remember pieces of you.
The visualization of your voice seems to
be the only crystal clear picture I can sum
up or come up with.

I remember your songs.
A fractured memory of what used to be
my favourite warm sound.
So clear and sweet,
my feet wandered to the beat and
instinctively reached to hold your hands:
"Come dance."

I remember dancing with you.
Slowly in the moonlight, swinging by the
sea, over golden-lit rainy streets, on top
of that hill overlooking the rest of the
world in their repeated realities.

PART III

I remember your lips.
The taste of too much chocolate
and hours of laughter.
I can taste them and feel
the outskirts of your smile when we'd kiss.

I remember the distinct outline of your jawline.
The bones along your cheeks
carving stories into my stomach,
up my legs, down my spine and I'd shiver.
I remember your whispers
down my neck and quiver.

I remember what we would do with me and you.
The way we'd change and rearrange
and wrap our bodies in warmth and lust
and moonlit, glittering stardust.

I remember waking up and being pulled,
lulled back closely into your chest,
and tracing your long breaths and sleepy heartbeat
with my cheek, on the lung that stuck out "just a little".

I remember that.
I remember pieces of you.

LITTLE TUNE

When the song
that's been silently
playing in the background
-for who knows how long-
suddenly grabs you and flings you back
a thousand miles per second to:

A year or so ago,
almost every night,
I'd be skipping
down the street
in the snow
to see you,
two feet away from my street,
singing these same words on repeat.
Funny how a little tune can bring me back to you.
Thinking of you.

Art: Jada Powell

FULL OF LIFE

You're not supposed
to see me like this.

"Like what?"

Like this. I'm a mess.

"I love you like this.
Life is messy
and right now,

you're full of it."

YOU, LIKE MOST NIGHTS, ARE IN MY THOUGHTS

Thinking of {you}
tonight, {like most}.
Thoughts of our {nights}
out chasing stars that {are}
shining brighter than the light {in}
your heart, that beats pressed to {my}
chest and fills my head with a million {thoughts}
of only you.

Art: Jada Powell

DUSTED PICTURES

You're in there, somewhere,
tied to the strings, hanging pictures that sting
and swing side to side, even when I sleep.

I can see you but you're older, faded and fainter.
I'm the painter but your colours are crooked
and your eyes are fixed
on a flat surface that doesn't exist.

Your limbs lose grip of the swinging strings
and suddenly they fall
far from their thin twine,
and though you don't yet know,
your landing will be fine.

You'll fall hard and fast
but within seconds, it will be in the past.
My strings will keep swinging
old dusted pictures of figures
that once were and were once
young "You"s and "I"s.

I eventually bounced back and caught grip of
the fallen photographs and dangling *used to be's*,
and though you'll never know,
I've tucked them away safely,
where they can't fall off of heartstrings.

Art: Hannah Ockenden

VICTORIA, BC

It's a funny feeling: falling in love with a place.
Every inch of me can feel and taste the scents
and sensations the ocean air brings to my face.
The heat that hits my arms and tickles my dimples,
until I'm smiling sunbeams out in every direction.
Miles away and still just steps from sinking my skin
into the sand and feeling waves roll and wash away the day.
I can hear the wind whispering through the birds,
the geese and the trees dancing in the dizzying breeze.
Even the buildings build blocks, sky-high in my head,
and watch as I walk from block to block
in my crystal clear imagination's eye.

SLICE OF EXISTENCE

Unashamed and untamed, you took my
hands and wrapped my worries in your arms.
And though I hear sirens and alarms,
and know we've both got storms the size of
this infinite galactic universe,
that we've somehow serendipitously slipped into
at the same precise slice of existence,

I'm fucking excited.

LITTLE UNIVERSE

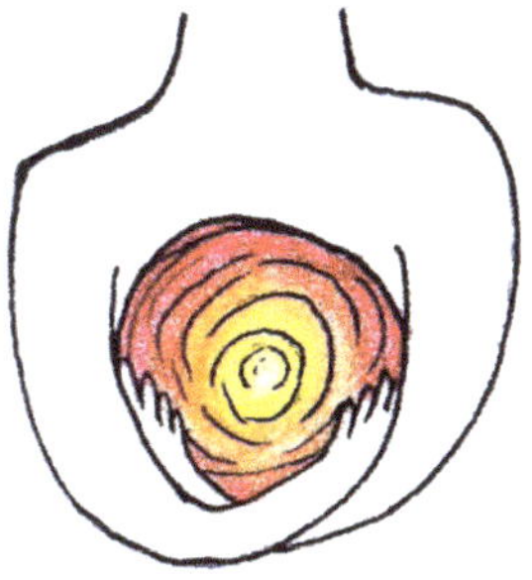

I trust in the little
universe
that makes up
me.

AGAIN & AGAIN

The one constant concept
in this world is:

The prospect of everlasting change.

So, it only makes sense
to do the same:

Reinvent yourself again
and again and again.

AN INCREDIBLE INCONVENIENCE

After six months
of falling through
galaxies,

he simply
wasn't right for her.

How
incredibly
Inconvenient.

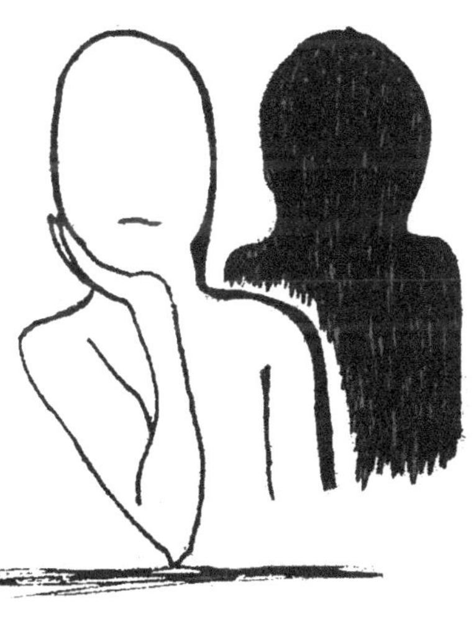

THROUGH THE EYES OF A LITTLE GIRL

When the light hit her,
the whole world shone with delight,
through the eyes of:

A little daisy.
A smooth river stone.
A cumulus cloud.
A wave or waft of air
through her cinnamon hair.

Every dandelion was a wish.
Shooting stars were a gift.
The sound of rain moved her feet.
The moon: a favourite treat;
a friend she could count on at every window.

Every item in her sight held
importance and delight,
and dangled in golden sunshine,
through the eyes of a little girl.

Art: Emma McEvoy

INSTANTLY

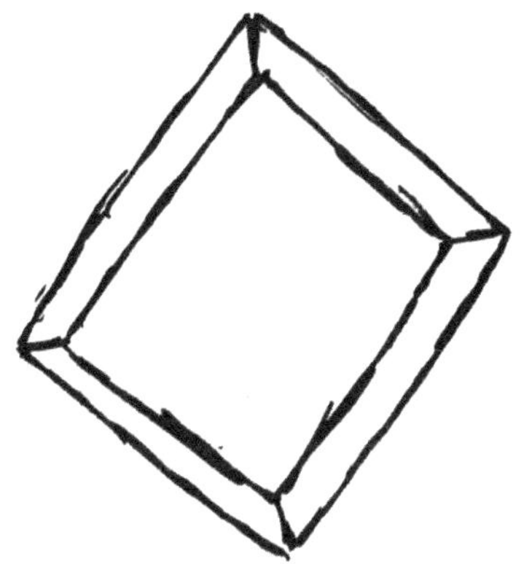

A picture of you.
A million emotions ran
through,
into,
and around me,
instantly.

Art: Hannah Ockenden

SWEET SERENDIPITY

Can someone
    simply
        explain to me
            how I got
                from there   to here,
                and then   to now,
                and where I was, to where I am today, somehow.

Art: Marten Sealy

MISS LITTLE ME

Your giggles and laughter
and skips through the banter
that break me today and tomorrow
are the answer.

Where did you go
with your innocent eyes
and your tiptoeing feet,
filling music with the beat of
your little dances?
I miss your careless innocence.
The fearless commitment:

To each day.
To each word.
To each hour of play.
In the fields.
In your room.
By the trees.
By the lake.
In the store.
Out the door.
At the shores of the world.

You never missed a single moment.
You'd grab it and embrace
every inch of its little existence
in your world of colour and craze.

I miss little me. Where on earth could
she be?

MIND FULL

Understanding a   FULL MIND
rather than a   MINDFUL   one.

POCKET OF SILENCE

I can't hear the silence we used to keep.
The one that felt so intimate. So safe. Precious.
If you dropped it, the walls caved in.
That sound is so rare.
I can't wait to find it, to hear it again.
Have you kept it with you this whole time?
Waiting for when you stand next to me, ready to
tap, tap, tap my shoulder and see me turn around.
That moment when I see you again for the first time
and everything STOPS
as you let out that precious pocket of silence.
It's so noisy out here.
I can't wait.
I hope you bring a few to pick and choose from.
We'll need them when we meet again.
So much to be accounted for in moments like those.
Moments where words simply won't do
and all you *can* do
is sit
in silence.
That simple, fragile silence.
I miss its sweet songs.
Bring us a few, won't you?

FEEL ALIVE

How curious it
is:
To live and
breathe
and one day
along the way,
find a thin
stain of sun,
and to suddenly
FEEL
entirely and
completely
ALIVE
all over again.

WISHFUL HEART

Suppose it's fair   to say I'm insane
after all of the hours I've sat up and saved up
the seconds and beckons of your sweet weapons
you've sharpened and shined with the tips of my
mind and my wandering, wavering, wishful
heart.
And yet, here we are, just as we were.
You're a wreck wreaking havoc,
but I can't defer and deter
from the thought of
what might
be mine.

WRITTEN & READ

Of course, it wasn't for nothing;
I met you for a reason.
The fact that you won't
get out of my head just means
there's more to this story than
what's already been written & read,
all neatly notated,
in a lined notebook,
and then washed and sloshed into
unrecognizable writing,
on the night that it rained
and removed the stains
of the never-ending new thoughts
I'd think up about you.

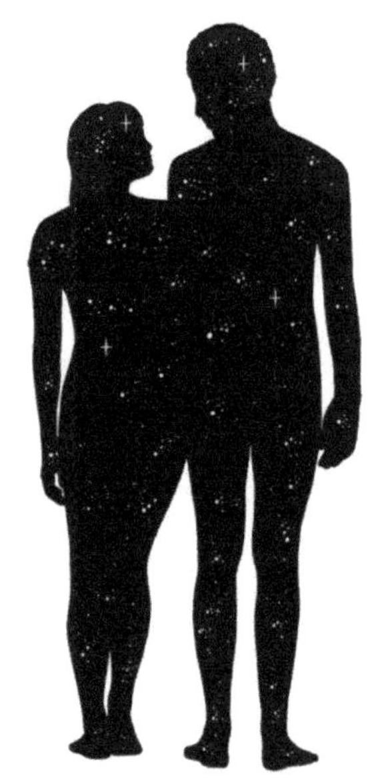

Art: @broken_isnt_bad

DISTANCE IN REALITY

Still here, my dear.
I've not gone anywhere.
In location I've stationed myself
far away, but between this
seemingly resistant distance,
in reality, you are
- every single day-
my first thought

when I wake,
when I bathe,
when I bake,
when I go out,
get home, eat,
sleep and repeat.
A split second in time,
and I'm back in your arms

on the floor,
in the car,
on the roof,
at the bar,
on the stairs,
in that chair,

piecing together
letters upon letters,
day after day,
after night, after fights
through a dim-lit shadow of
something's not right.

REARRANGING SPACE

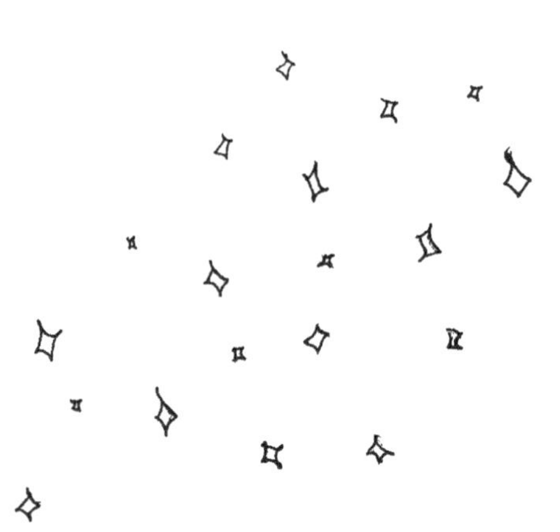

Some say
it makes them feel small
to see the whole picture.
Somehow,
I always feel bigger
glancing up at
the glittering glow
of faraway galaxies,
slowly growing,
forever changing,
rearranging space
before our eyes.

REACHING ACROSS THE SILENT ROOM

I'm sorry that I sit back and stare
and make all of the pieces of you that I can see
flare up in flames I don't dare or care to understand.
I tear you to pieces before learning your name.
I'm sorry that I've made up my mind
about how you spend your time,
and can't seem to find a single second to spend
getting to share what it is those flames feel like,
or how it feels to burn from ashes and aches
and shakes I'll never stare down.
From bubbles and boils my fingers won't ever coil or cool
with anything but ice cold comments,
from a concept I create inaccurately, as an outside eye.
Before you open your mouth to speak and tweak
the already elongated explanation of who you are in my head,
you've got labels of length and lucid dreams
dangling above your head, that I have somehow managed to
makeshift into your own personalized mold.
I'm sorry is all.
I'm sorry that I sit back and stare instead of
reaching across the silent room
to take your hand and meet your eyes,
and smile back at the truth of who you are.
It's nice to meet you. The real you.
Sorry for the version I decided was true.
I like you better when you tell it this way: your way.
So, for the first time: I'm sorry.

THE LITTLE VOICES

Listen.
The little voices you keep hearing
are probably saying something worth listening to.

Whisper.
Not every voice
has made itself known
by being thrown across
continents and seas.

Sometimes
the most important words
are short and sweet:
just a simple, silent whisper,
slipping between tiny lips
that pucker up and press out
just enough breath to make
a minuscule murmur.

Listen.
And remember:
not all words or thoughts are big and strong
but all play a part in what comes along.

SUBTEXT

I see space between,

a place between,

the words you say

and the words you mean.

GROWING UP

When they describe "growing up",
they somehow skip all of the in-betweens
when "What does it all mean?"
is the one thing separating awake and a dream.
The made-up, mindless princess and queens
shitting on your inner self-esteem.
The steaming cycle and circle of head rush
and heartaches and head throbs
and night shakes. The:
Who the hell am I
and why the hell can't I
just be here right where I
am sitting, instead I
stick myself so far into my head,
allow all of my demons to stitch and thread
every word that I've said,
and will say,
until hopefully, one day,
I will suddenly feel like me again:
Somewhat tame again.
Sane again.
Why don't they ever mention this part?
When can I go back to the start
and listen more clearly
and hear sincerely
why they won't ever mention this part?

TO THE SEA

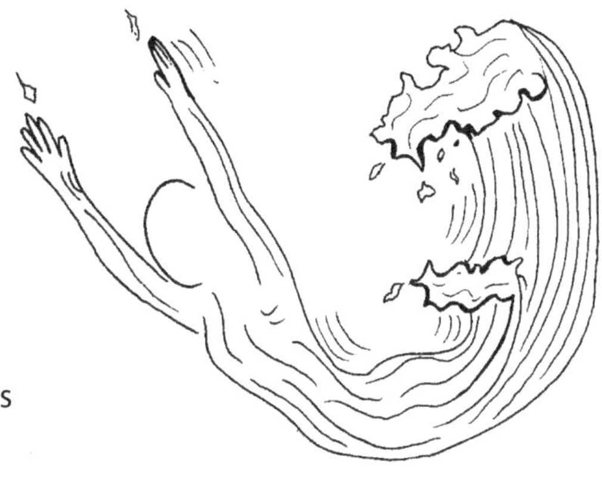

I was born in the mountains
and fled to the sea,
because some part of me
yearned for infinity;

endless freedom in every direction,
the constant, consistent connection
to the earth and air, the sky and sand,
standing with the edge of the world in my hand.

CONSTANT DISCOVERY

I'm in love with people I have yet to meet
and places I have yet to see.
But, here I am in places with people
that did not always exist to me.
And thus, it's become quite clear recently,
that this life is a constant discovery.

Art: @broken_isnt_bad

LITTLE MIRACLES

Tell me we're not all little miracles,
laughing through another irreplaceable day
on what could perfectly realistically be
a star spinning through infinity.

Art: Jenny Hawes

SLOW DANCING IN A THUNDERSTORM

She sort of wondered
why it all happened so quickly.
One moment, you're spinning through infinity,
the next, slow dancing in a thunderstorm,
slipping further into the unknown,
as time prances in distant directions around you.
You'll have a glimpse of connection
when suddenly,
miles of mountains, lakes,
and rivers separate you
but the plane never took off.
In the morning, you're a sleepy six-year-old,
slumped in your mother's arms
and that night you're flying home
for the fifth Christmas since you
graduated, got a job, bought a car,
and crossed the country
in search of your twenty-year-old self.
Sun's down and the stars show you pieces of yourself
you'd have otherwise left forgotten and faded.
Sun rises and you're on top of that mountain
you always wanted to climb and can't remember
the path that put you there.
The view is beautiful but barely lasts long enough to take a
picture, that will sit in stillness until you mount it on the wall
and the mouths of memory recount it all.

Art: Hannah Ockenden

YOURS, SINCERELY

I wanted to shower you in abundance
the instant after entrance into
this complete trance
you've danced me anew
and swept me into,

while the old thoughts,
the lost thoughts,
the wandering spots in my mind,
that I could never find a rhyme
or a reason for having or breathing,
suddenly make way
for a fresh new season.

You walk through the door
and the shores go for miles,
and the smiles last for aisles of waves,
page after page after page.
I've been writing about you for days.
I've missed this feeling, you've found me anew,
and for that, I sincerely thank you.

INTOXICATED

I'm a whole lot of love for you
and somehow entirely lost
in the blue scattered lines
between what I want
and what is true.
In front of me and you
is a dotted,
spotted,
polka-dotted
line of *ifs*
and *buts*
and *maybes*
and *whats*
and *hows*
and *whys*
and constant smiles
with sober eyes.
Intoxicated legs
that stumble and fumble
into my arms,
falling too fast to catch.
A break.
A breath.
Catch me if I slip,
tip into his mess.

Art: Hannah Ockenden

THE POETRY YOU SEE

There's a lot more to
you and me
than the poetry you see,
all dotted and lined
with organized rhymes
and eloquent thoughts
with words we were taught.
It's what hides in between
that shows what I mean.
Our movements in motion
and all the commotion
between what makes sense
from the outside pretence
that everything is as it seems.

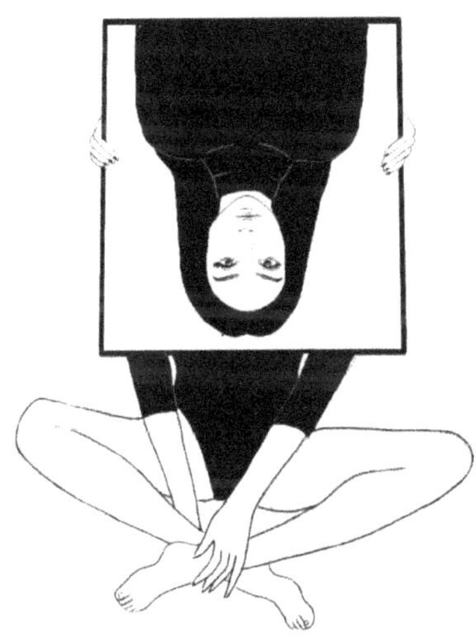

Art: @_danijelaa_

SEVEN VOICES

Me and
the seven voices in my head
used to be friends.
Now it depends
on life's little factors
added up to
detract and react to.
Some days, they love me.
Some days, they hate me.
And frankly,
I don't know how to convince
the seven voices in my head
that on any given day,
it's still just vulnerable me underneath.

TOUCH GROUND

Haven't felt my foot touch ground
in well over a while.
Been hovering over the earth and the dirt,
when suddenly,
the weight of the world reminds me:
gravity is not the only thing that ties me
back to the surface of reality.

I LIKE THAT...

I like that
you know when I'm around,
'cause you've memorized the sound
of my heart,

anxiously beating,
humbly meeting
your nerves
in the middle of this room,
bursting with chemistry,
trust, and anticipated lust.

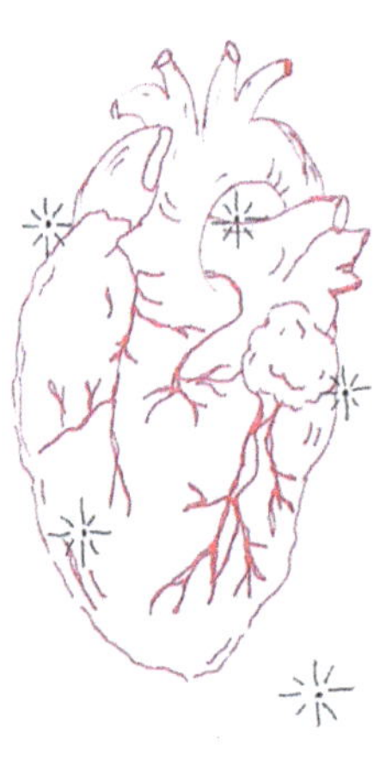

Art: Mikaela Kruse

You know those days
when you

feel
like a
single drop
of rain?

Alone, cold and outcast from
the universe's coloured storms.

On those days,
it's important to pay close attention to
those who find you,
cover you in sunshine's warmth
and remind you of your worth.
It's those few who really, truly, love you.

THOSE DAYS

IF I SAT THE WHOLE WORLD DOWN

If I sat the whole world down
and handed them nothing but
a pen and a piece of plain paper...
If I asked them to sit down and jot down
whatever is in their mind,
for less than a quarter of an hour...
No two pieces would ever turn out the same.
No two minds would create the same tower
of untamable thoughts.
I think about that a lot.

Art: Hannah Ockenden

ECHOED LAUGHTER

I hear the echoes of laughter along the mountain ranges,
similar to that of children's exchanges,
singing and swinging time between them.

It's a game they play
from day to day.
While the sun is up,
the hours are lost
in fun amidst the silent hum
of absolute serenity.
As the sun tucks under the lowest peak,
they softly sing themselves to sleep.

Art: Karly Fredrickson

WHAT YOU SOUND LIKE

You didn't say anything
and neither did I.
It's what you didn't say
that's caught my eye.

My wonder and attention
are distracted by the motion
of a silent language between us-
our bodies speaking in chorus.

I'm obsessed with what you sound like.

FINE, THANKS

Found her lying there,
half-smiling.
Sandy blonde hair.
The way it came tumbling,
fumbling down her soft-spoken face.
Tracing footprints down her cheeks
covered in misunderstandings
with landings of salty streaks.
Waterfalls
shaking into place the way she
felt inside the five-foot-high
opaque mask over grey skies.

How are you?

"Fine, thanks."

Art: Jenny Hawes

WHAT DO YOU SEE?

Finally coming to realize:
clearing out the **inside**
does in turn clean up
the outlook, output and **outside** world.

Everything inward spills
and fills our vision.
A daily decision,
making or breaking
your intake of the outside world.

What do you see?

Art: Sidney Cummings

BUTTERFLY WINGS

I wanted to tell you

"I love you"

today…

but the letters

got caught in

butterfly wings.

TRUE BEAUTY

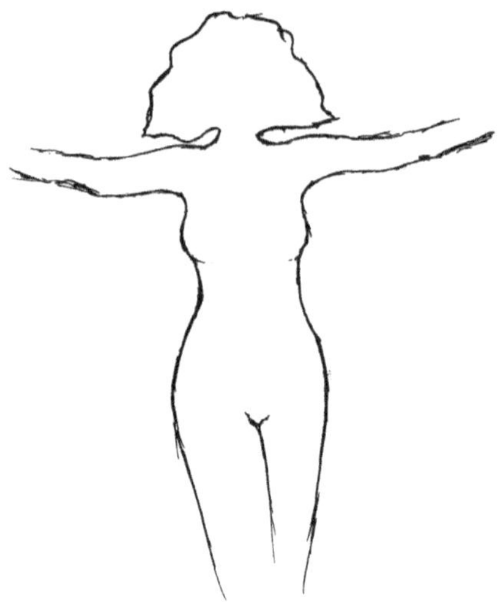

The hours women put themselves through
simply seeking to be approved,
construed as
a "true beauty",
astounds me.

You are what is underneath those hours:
True, beautiful, you.

Art: Hannah Ockenden

BROKEN SILHOUETTE

It seems I've taken it upon myself
to pick up the pieces you've been tearing off,
and somehow put you back together again.
Though, I can't seem to keep up:
for every piece I put up, you drop double.
My hands are full
but your broken silhouette sheds incessantly.

Art: @sidraws_

ALONE TOGETHER

Waiting in a room, alone, on their own,
just the two of them, together.

She already knew he wanted to,
but still pretended not to.
He wore it in his hands and feet,
the way they tip-tapped every beat
of restless room between them,
building up unbearable chemistry.

The electricity pleads.
His knee gently knocks hers,
and instantly,
they speed fall fifty feet away
and stay, solid in place,
in case of uncontrollable outbursts
that poke and pry from their insides.

Their shared silence screams
"LUST!" over rooftops,
and though she knows he wants to,
she sweetly pretends not to.

Waiting in a room, alone, on their own,
just the two of them, together.

Art: Hannah Ockenden

UNFATHOMABLE

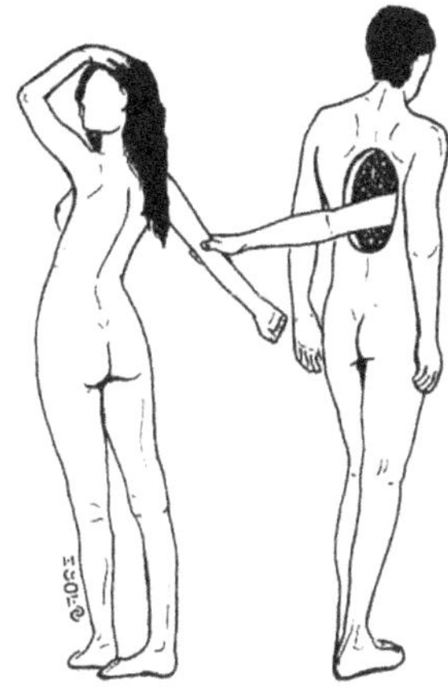

It's easier to grasp

the unfathomable task

of

forgetting you

when you're far away.

Art: @fiorediop

TO MY LUNA

Gypsy sisters holding hands,
skipping through the sand,
demanding more daylight
while the sun sets and breaks
their laughter just long enough
for a speechless moment of awe.

Gypsies in the snow,
singing softly adieu.
"I'll be seeing you" again, ma belle.
Dancing on tiptoes
while their cold noses
rest on shoulders
who've held them longer
than the years
they've known each other.

Gypsies in the wind,
hearing whispers
of each other's wonders
from their sister, Ocean's waves,
keeping them in touch through
synchronized tales.

Gypsies in the moonlight,
in the sunlight,
over dunes and lakes,
rivers and moons.

We've travelled this whole world together
through our many lives, my sister.
My soul is in your eyes and yours in mine
until the time we next sit together,
and fill this room, once more,
with our sweet gypsy laughter.

Art: Jo Barnes

INTERTWINE

Touching him with my stardust fingers,
leaving a glow to show
where my lingering gaze
has grazed
and stays,
longing and wanting
to intertwine
my light with his fire.

I WON'T

I'm incredibly aware of your absence,
your lack of presence
in my immediate life.

I wish I was unable to hurt you.
To love you,
and tell you.
And for it to not send you
spinning in a confusing tizzy.

Wish I could sit with you.
Kiss you.
Hold you.
Tell you all of the ways I still think of you.

But I won't.
For your heart.
Your hurt heart.
I won't.

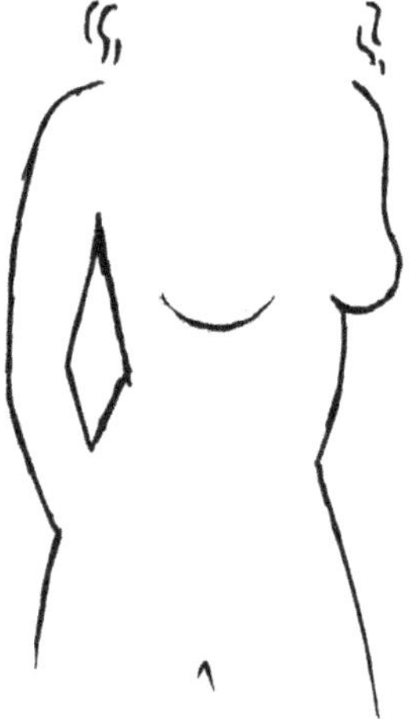

Art: Hannah Ockenden

FORGET IT

And you tell me:
you're jealous of the rain that touches my skin,
        jealous of the dreams I sleep with,
        jealous of the men I've never loved.

        If that's the only confirmation of affection
        you have for me: **forget it.**

YOUR DARKNESS PREVAILS

The game you played
kept me so far away,
in hotel rooms apart,
where the unclear,
smeared outskirts
of your guarded heart
couldn't get hurt.

But then you'd call,
once the lined up bottles
stopped numbing the pain,
and the green smoke
covering every inch of your lungs
finally choked denial's tongue.

And once again, you'd beat in your brain
with the same old worthless tales,
proving to my frail heartstrings,
above all else: your darkness prevails.

A MILLION TIMES

I've fallen in love
with the moon a million times.
I hope she doesn't get tired
of me romanticizing in her starlight,
wishing on meteor showers and hours of
extended glances into infinite skies.

COLLARBONES

I often dive into
the pools
your
collarbones
carved into
my memory.

GLITCH

The light switch
two-faced
loving bitch
with a glitch
to itch and stitch
burdens which
aren't hers to fix.

Art: @ma_goa

LET ME SEE

Most people
haven't really
met me,
just a version
I let people see.

Art: Hannah Ockenden

MY PERSONAL COLLECTION

Welcome to, "My Personal Collection":
A walking, talking exhibition of
twenty-two years worth of artifacts.

1. A Crooked Smile,
a single-sided triplet
of dimpled ripples,
right under her lip,
that twists her mouth
a little to the side
when she smiles sincerely.

2. Even Eyes
that change colour
in summer and spring,
and darken to
welcome winters in.

3. A Tooth
twisting to cuddle
- a little too closely-
the one right next to it.

4. A Non-Existent Upper Lip
when she laughs.

5. Baby Fuzz
outlining her hairline,
in constant contradiction
of what direction to fall in.

6. A Forehead Scar
from her two-year-old fall,
flat on her face.

7. Hair.
Everywhere.
That she cares not to share
with anyone,
until the falling follicles
accumulate and cause a ruckus
between the roommates.

8. An Uncommonly High Belly Button
that sticks out of
every high-waisted pair of
pants on the planet.

9. A Lower Back Mole
continuing to grow,
more and more,
little by little,
as the years come and go.

10. Knees
that knock each other off
course and challenge her balance.

11. Stretch Marks
that show where she changed most
between then and now, somehow.

12. Burn Marks
on either wrist,
from the kitchen adventures
that always ended fatally for the food.

13. A "Strawberry" Red Birthmark
at the top of her neck,
hiding under
the brunette she grew into.

14. A Recovered Collarbone
from falling, at only six years,
down a flight of stairs, wearing
nothing but mother's ski boots.

15. A Doodled Idea
eternally ingrained
on her upper spine,
of her holding onto the moon.

16. Scapulas
that refuse to stay in place,
and instead,
stick straight out,
like shark fins in space.

17. A Finger Width of Room
between her ribs and hips,
which inhibits full flexion
in any given direction.

18. A Tea-Bag-Sized Spider Bite
on her right calf
from a careless critter
who came too close,
and a doctor who failed to help
in any other way than
a *Tetley Green Tea* bag.

19. Fragile Ankles
that have taken turns
rolling completely out of place,
too many times to count.

20. Hobbit Hairs
on terribly ticklish toes,
who once almost broke dad's nose.

21. Inked Stars
on the inside of her right ear,
of the 3 best friends she holds dear.

22. Waves
on the left inner foot,
after swimming in the Turkish sea
and hanging on for dear life to the straps
of a striped purple parachute
while sprinting off a mountain, full speed.

YOUR CONSTELLATIONS

I spent more time,
in our shared time,
studying the constellations
perfectly placed on your face

than all of the hours in my life
spent staring up at the stars,
romancing and dancing in space.

Art: Hannah Ockenden

A LITTLE MESS

Life's meant to be *a little* messy.
Like when you spill your hot coffee
all over his new white button-up shirt,
you get to meet *a little* more of him,
and hear him say
a little more than the formal:
"Thank you and have a nice day."
Now you are
"The Girl Who Ruined My White Shirt"
and every time you walk in
he'll giggle, just *a little*.
He'll memorize your drink
so every time you visit
he'll have it ready,
and you'll giggle just *a little*.
You'll buy him a new shirt
and learn his name, to make amends.
Now you're the girl
he buttons up his new white shirt for
a little nervously
to take out for the fourth coffee this week.

Life's *a little* messy.
Let it be;
you never know what a blessing
a little mess might be.

Art: Baran Ayguler

EXPERIENCE YOURSELF

Perhaps
this is a period of time
when you simply
get to experience yourself -
in however many ways
that could mean.

Art: @notart.jpeg

SHAPE OF YOU

If my past
had a shadow,
it would be
the shape of you.

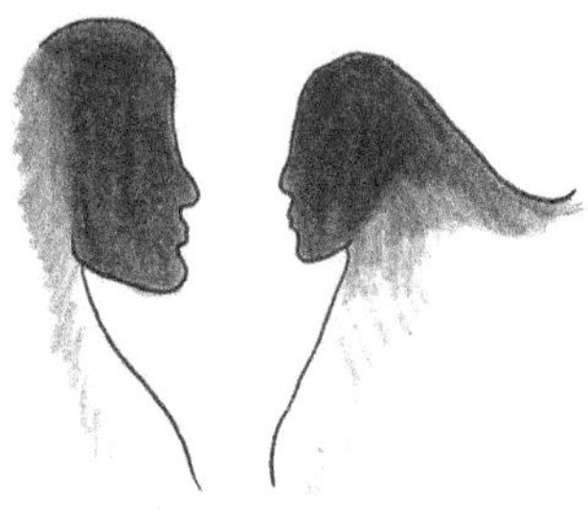

Art: Jada Powell

I COULD DRINK

I wish your scent
was a substance
I could drink.
Fill my lungs and liver
simultaneously
with intoxicating
tingles down my spine
every single time
you walk through
the door.

Art: Hannah Ockenden

SUPERPOWER

I believe everybody has
a superpower.
Mine happens to be
finishing a full-sized
chocolate bar,
5 seconds before
my foot reaches
the car door
while leaving the
grocery store.

Art: Jada Powell

THE DRIVE

The night we started
the drive that left you broken-hearted
I swear I had no idea
we would end up in a
whirlwind of a
thousand speechless conversations
that would end in separation
over continents and oceans.

Art: Jada Powell

AMONG THE MIX

Remember to surrender to
the simple side of you
that shouts for *silence*
among the mix
of social cues.

Art: Lilla Clara

HELPLESSNESS

Helplessness is the strangest feeling.
Your hands suddenly have no purpose,
reaching continuously for temporary relief,
distraction from the twisting, shifting thoughts,
going back and forth between
the optimist's pessimistic feelings
sinking into your stomach.
"Should I eat? Sleep?"
Awake without reason,
pacing in circles around
the food you made without appetite.
Suddenly the plate is cleaned and put away,
you lapped around the living room 5 times,
ate the entire jar of hazelnut butter,
repainted the door, scrubbed the floor,
and don't remember what brought you to the balcony.
Endless ringtones and elevator music on the other end
while "on hold" for what seems like forever.
You shower 3 times.
The third round's cold water
doesn't pass through the adrenaline into your nerves.
All you want to know is if he's okay.
On the other side of the world,
in an ambulance,
with a driver you don't know,
an injury you can't see and no one saying anything concrete.
All you can do is wait.
Helplessness is the worst feeling.

EFFORTLESSLY

Sometimes I sit back and smile
at all of the pondering and
purposeless worrying I've done,
while all of the things
that I've asked for and received
have been spinning around me,
effortlessly.

JUST BECAUSE

Just because you're family
doesn't mean
they know you care.
The thoughts in your head
are not transparent.
Show it.
Say it.
Write it.
Mean it.

Art: Hannah Ockenden

LIFE'S ADVENTURE

Imagine reading a book about somebody's life,
where every day remained the same.
Stagnant events occurring in scheduled slots
over and over again, week in and week out.
Every instance, perfectly on time,
exactly as expected, perfectly predicted.

After ten pages, you'd be sick
of the stillness,
of the ceaseless certainty.
You'd yearn for something -
ANYTHING new.
No story is meant
to remain the same.
We are meant to
age, grow, conquer,
lead, love, learn,
break, fall, follow,
embrace our fate
and make countless mistakes.
That's the joy of life's adventure:
You never know what's around the
corner.

Art: @laurenmaria.b

UNFURLED

She's scared to let people in.
Where to begin
with all of the
unfurled feelings inside,
that, with someone else
watching,
have nowhere to hide.

Art: @hello_hann_

CHOOSE CAREFULLY

Some wines pour tears down our cheeks.
Some drag us out of our sleep.
Some take our minds to fantasies.
Some drag us back to memories.
Some wines make us forget where we are.
Some shut off who we are.
Some wines pull us to the present.
Some make us entirely transparent.
Some turn every hormone on high.
Some make us quiet and shy.
Some taste like strawberry shakes.
Some bring regretful mistakes.
Some we'll buy again and again.
Some we haven't got the money to spend.
Some make us cry from laughter.
Some make us apologize after.
Some wines are for everybody.
And some simply aren't for me.
Choose carefully. Which one will it be?

Art: Hannah Ockenden

WHAT I'M USED TO

I seem to be attracted to

anyone who sounds similar to

anything other than what I'm used to.

READY

He loved you
so much more
than you were ready for.

Walking down a moonlit
sandy seaside
with the sound of the shore
getting caressed
and undressed
more and more.

DEFINE SEXY

HEY STRANGER

Hi.
You
don't yet
know me.
But one day,
I will love you
more than anybody.
Thought I'd put down in writing:
I very much look forward to us meeting.

Art: Jada Powell

Why do we place
our whole worth
in the palms of a person
we met only a moment ago,
who knows us better
than they know themselves?

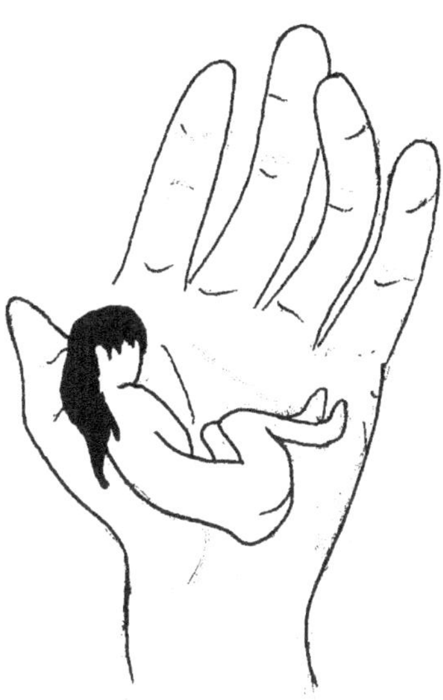

GOOD QUESTION

PERHAPS IN A DREAM

If not in reality,
perhaps in a dream.

You swear
we've never met before.
True: while we sleep,
we cannot create a face
we have never seen.
Therefore,
I swear
we've met before.

Art: Jada Powell

There was something magic
about the way the sunlight
sparkled off of every spinning

drop

of
rain,
while
she

danced, laughing,
barefoot that day.

MAGIC

YET YOU LINGER

You left
yet
you linger,
longer than
the everlasting lullaby
of your laughter,
looping consistently,
lulling me to sleep
without you by my side.

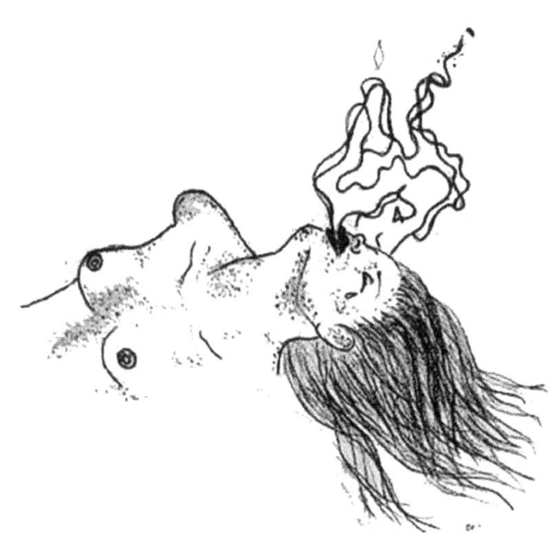

FOR A MOMENT YOU WOULD KNOW

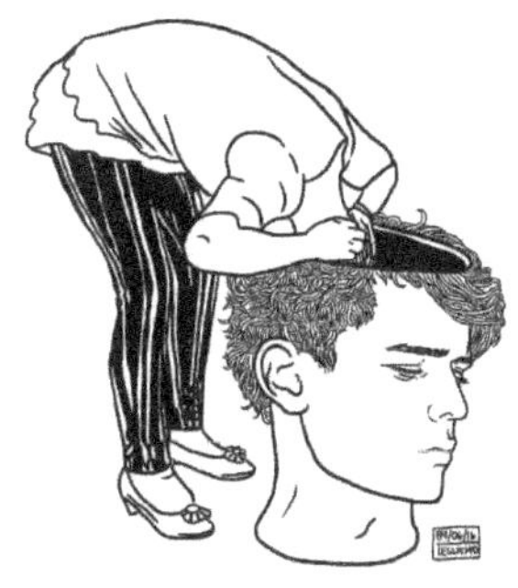

If you slipped into my mind
FOR A MOMENT
and connected every dot between
the synapses of thoughts
and figures behind every feeling
and reflection of the words
I'm speaking to you now,
YOU WOULD KNOW
that nothing you're perceiving
as an outward onlooker of this experience
is about you. So when you hear
IT'S NOT YOU,
now you know,
IT'S
everything going on
inside of every inch of
ME.

Art: @oh_long_leslie

HOW'D I GET SO LUCKY

The fact that this is where my mind is at
shows in full, permanent proof
how very far my mental state
has bended and mended
over the course of 9.5 months,
on an island I didn't know existed
two years before today.
How'd I get so lucky?

A flipbook full of faces and places
over 11 countries, and continents
across oceans from where I call home.
A cup full of dreams
I didn't know I had
until taking my first sip.
A pen spilling pages
of phrases filling
the thoughts I thought I'd lost
in writing, helping me find my way.
How'd I get so lucky?

A continuous adventure
I often have no control over
and always end up in a blunder
of new found chapters to read over;
a page turner for the autobiographical author.
How'd I get so lucky?

Art: Sidney Cummings

I WONDER

I wonder if the universe is a friend of mine.
Perhaps we've even met before,
shaken hands, kissed both cheeks.
Good morning. Bonjour. Buongiorno. Buenos dias.
How are you? Comment ça va? Come stai? Como estas?
What an infinite answer that must be
for someone who's beginning never ends.
I bet your eyes tell every memory of human history.
How complex it must feel
to pass by every person on the street
and instantly be filled with every piece of their past
and every second of the rest of their lives,
the minute you lock eyes.

I wonder if the universe ever curls up in the corner
to close her eyes and stop the clock
just long enough to clear her mind.
I wonder what she's thinking.
I wonder where she's sitting,
planting seeds for every minute
of every living, breathing piece of life
that will touch this lifetime.
In a coffee shop? On the clouds?
Swimming through waves?
Might be meditating with monks or
skipping through New York City.
Maybe in a taxi, on her way to see
Earth, Wind, Fire and Water,
the four friends she made up
to fill this little toy of hers.

Art: Mikaela Kruse

I wonder what she does for fun.
Does she sing when she spins the sun
through her untouchable fingertips?
Can she two-step to a tune?
Is she entirely tone-deaf
and yet entirely willing
to belt out the wrong words innocently
to all the music she hears us make.

I wonder what she looks like.
Do constellations fall from her lips
every time she speaks?
Do tsunamis hit when she surrenders
to the fears in her head,
or are they the rivers of her tears?
Are the colours of her irises
the cumulation of every lake, sea and ocean
in a set of eyes?
The freckles on each cheek,
a desert's depth of detail.
Her cheekbones,
each mountain range in the Alps,
cut clean and screaming "Unbeatable beauty".
I wonder how many dimples she has when she smiles
like ripples on water for endless days,
and her laughter sprinkling galaxies
over salted seas.

I wonder if she prefers the Sun or the Moon,
seeing, as a celestial,
she can pick and choose according to the mood.
I wonder if she likes ice cream or sorbet,
if she digs man buns and Cabernet.
I wonder if she lives by the sea,
overlooking mountains,

or hidden from the rest of us,
in a dreamy wooden house, up a willow tree.

I wonder if I met the universe
what she'd say to me,
how her voice would be,
what the shape of her body looks like,
if her anger bites,
if she's ticklish or uptight,
if she has nicknames that only her closest stars know,
if she parties on our polka-dot planet with thunder and
lightning as her lights.
I wonder if she ever feels alone.

I wonder if she's vegan or sensitive to wheat,
if she prefers the pronoun "They"
and is a newly uncloseted gay.
I wonder what size shoes she wears,
and if she likes milk chocolate over dark,
if she ever sleeps,
and what happens when she dreams.
I wonder if she ever doubts her unfathomable abilities
with limitless possibilities.
I wonder if she shares my sense of humor,
if she juggles planets in her spare time,
or knits sweaters for extended family
she sees coming in the future.

I wonder what her pet peeves are
and if stars colliding is her version of fireworks.
I wonder if her middle name is Intuition
and her last name is Indecision.
I wonder if she procrastinates our fate
and we perceive it as "life's unpredictability".
I wonder if she paints a sunset every night

and if she drinks her coffee black.
I wonder if she wakes up every morning smiling,
knowing everything is unfolding
exactly as it's meant to be.

I wonder if the universe
is watching me write this,
giggling, because she knows,
as well as I do,
that she's very much a part of me
and that all of these thing I'm wondering,
I already know the answers to.
    I wonder.
        I wonder.
            I wonder.

SHINE

I've always preferred the night.
It's then when you see the ones
who really shine.

ISN'T IT MARVELLOUS?

She twists and turns like the river's banks,
bashing against bold rocks,
facing the freezing cold
and never skipping a beat.
Flowing farther away from
past falsehoods and two-faced canvases
filling up too much space.
It never stops.
Isn't it marvelous?
The eye never darts away
and that same speed and flow
will last until the sun is low.
How many minuscule drops
have *splished* and *splashed*
their little feet across those slippery slopes
is unknown to the eye of the onlooker.
It all just passes milestone after stone
with such ease and grace, leaving a trace of
everflowing followers in their footsteps.
Such power in their pattern.
So much energy circling and cycling, again and again.
Not one minuscule drip drop topples over the same spot.
They scatter and clump together but never fall over.
Never stopping. Everflowing. Taking every corner.
Cutting through every fork in the road without hesitation.
What a gift that would be - to let go and be free.
Isn't it marvelous?

You've somehow
slipped past my psyche
and tightened
your grip between
breaths,
grasping onto
one sharp lasting
gasp,
choking the
oxygen
filling my
lungs,
stopping my
tongue
from speaking
merciful sympathy you
never deserved from me.
It feels like **you're choking me**.

LET GO OF ME

DANCING FINGERTIPS

I sat, staring at
her dancing
fingertips

and the world
sort of slipped
away
for a second

or however many
it was until she
turned around and
smiled at me,

lost in a world
she'd made around
me.

A MERE REFLECTION

A mere reflection in a mirror
says nothing about a person, my dear.
Nowadays ladies wear
and tear their hair and face for hours
before showing in a public place.
They say a picture paints a thousand words
but our miraculous, mutated molecules
have lost their zest and crest
of family earned,
carefully crafted genes,
by sitting, staring at ourselves in the glass
and painting it, all over,
with layer after layer
of powder and brush and plastic lip lush
to look like every other.
The picture you get
of them "perfecting" how they appear
says not a million, but
one thing, my friend
: fear.

Show your skin.
Show your stars.
Show the tales of your scars.
Fear the loss of freedom
in delighting
in who you're meant to be.
Forget the box built by society
squishing your bones in anxiety,
painting your gifts

until they're unrecognizable,
impossible to see.
Breathe and let be
the face you were given,
smile and set free
the body you were given.
Imagine the amount of unbeatable variety
humankind holds; unimaginable beauty.
If only we'd remove our masks and
show what we're made of. Tangible facts:
Skin. Bones. Flesh. Hair. Birthmarks.
Fat. Nails. Wrinkles. Dimples. Scars. Moles.
Oil. Wax. Salt. Sweat. Tears. Blood.
We are all unfathomably
unique miracles,
made to
breathe deep,
cry aloud,
laugh until our tears
fill our dimples with salted pools
and we ache in the pit of our cores.

We are so much more
than the simple outer layer
shown on our pores.

A mere reflection in a mirror
says nothing about a person, my dear.

ONLY UNKNOWNS

So many uncertainties
slipping through
my psyche,
and still,
I pursue the path
of only unknowns.

Art: @oh_long_leslie

THE FILLING FEELING OF LAUGHTER

I think I'm falling for the feeling of laughter
filling every inch of flailing limb,
while the fun facts,
forcing me back and forth,
spill from lips
of friendly, frequented faces.
I rarely roll on the floor
unless it's around you,
roaring with endorphin-inducing symptoms:
rock-solid wit,
the best belly ache,
and sore, smiling cheeks,
time and time again,
with you, my friend.

Art: Hannah Ockenden

If we met today,

would you feel
the same way?
Would we fall the
same as we did then?

If we passed on the street,
would you stop and greet
or turn the corner
to avoid disorder?

Would you be alone
or with another?
Would she know me
from your words?
What picture have you painted?
What words have
coloured me in a stranger's mind?

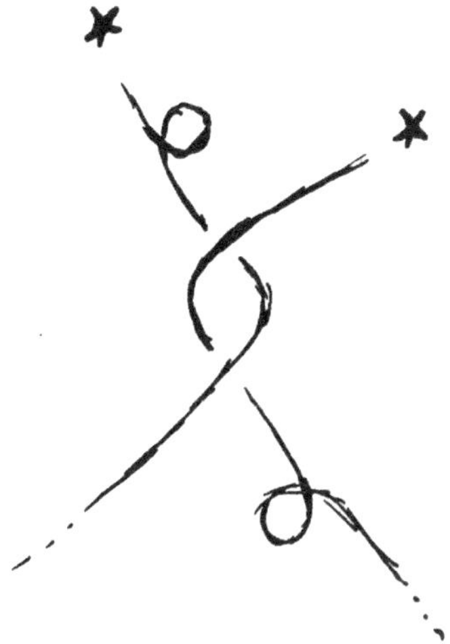

IF WE MET TODAY

Art: Hannah Ockenden

WHAT HE SEES

I'm sitting, staring at a man who can't see.
Wondering why we waste our gift of sight
on screens to scroll through peoples'
edited past versions of themselves,
rather than taking the time to look and see
every single detail on a face and count
each freckle or dimpled ripple of a smile we see,
each and every day.

What a gift we were given.
How often we forget
how precious our senses are.
We take for granted the simplicities and intricacies
and hardly even look around anymore.
We waste so much time staring down
at things that have already happened
and lose what's constantly shifting,
shaping, changing around us.
The colours, the scents, the sights, the sounds.
The simple act of feeling a fresh flower's petal,
breathing in the scent of summer saying goodnight,
listening to the sound of someone we love laughing,
like for a moment, nothing else in the world matters.

I'm sitting, staring at a man who can't see
and he has such a pleasant smile on his face.
I wonder, if asked to paint a picture,
what he sees in his mind
in this one moment in time.

SPEND SOME TIME IN OUTER SPACE

You need to sit and stare at stars
to understand the way I think.
Spend some time in outer space,
exploring stardust's presence in every place.
Come back when your eyes start to glow
and your spirit wishes regularly
on shooting stars, flying in every direction.
Find me when you see
we're all just stardust, really.

Art: Hannah Ockenden

SPILLED

A sip.
Too much,
too soon;
I spilled over
the moon.
Too hot,
too dry;
waterfalls in July.
I slipped,
you sighed;
you weren't
the right guy.

Art: Jada Powell

ACROSS MY PILLOW

I used to sit and stare for hours
into infinite oceans of eyes
across my pillow.
I used to sleep on my right side
and you, on your left,
so we could puzzle piece together,
facing each other,
while the other slept.
Usually, you.
I'd watch, totally mused
by the idea that
endless oceans awaited
behind tired eyes
that would
and could open
at any minute,
across my pillow.

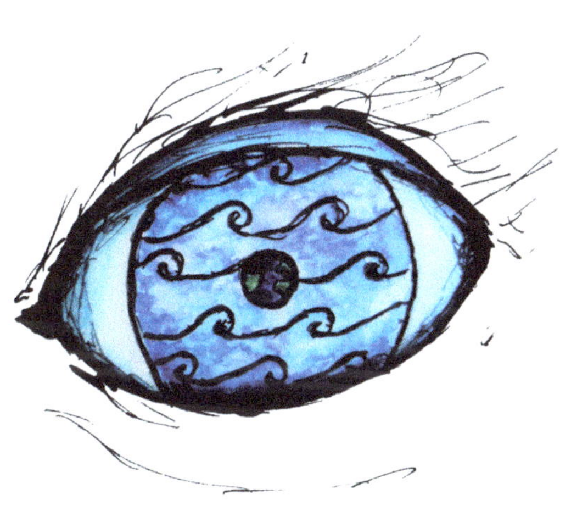

Art: Hannah Ockenden

SLIPPED AWAY

Isn't it surreal
how it all passes
faster by the day,
and suddenly sunlight skips away,
and twenty years have slipped away?

Art: Olivia Garstin-Collier

ON THE BACK OF MY NECK

There's a permanent mark
on the curve of my spine,
where the nerves intertwine
and feed up my back
with a twist and a turn,
and a small interject,
where your lips left their name
on the back of my neck.

PIECE OF ME

I've sent you
this piece of me
to rest my uneasy
heartbeat
upon your cheek
and let you in
on what you seek.

Art: @_augustobm

MAKE ROOM

There's a
secret garden inside -
that you hide
under years
of your unspent fears -
waiting to bloom,
if only
you'd make room.

Art: Maisie Rose

LITTLE WING

I wish the wings
my mother gave me
when she named me
flew as quickly
as my thoughts of you.

Art: Hannah Ockenden

BETWEEN THESE PAGES

Some nights,
I sleep between these pages
of chapters, all before this,
to read through all the places
where our lives once interlaced.

Some nights,
I sleep between the pages,
these paper-thin walled places
bring me back to you.

Every line.
Every word.
Every comma, dot. Exclaim!
Every letter's jagged edge
or hyphenated-aim.

Every single structured frame
- alphabetically,
phonetically, with
rhythmic intricacy -
brings me back to you.

And I'd rather sleep between these pages   than without you.

Art: Tara Nareshwar

MOONLIT MEMORIES

A part of you resides in me
and takes me back to melodies
of rainy street lights,
moonlit memories:

Swinging sweet jazz,
a saxophone blaring out summer romance,
a dance, cheek to cheekbone,
chiseling midnight marbled edges into my mind.

FAVOURITE TIME OF DAY

When the rain stains every street and windowpane
a golden midnight glow,
and the only sound along the puddled sidewalk
is the friendly neighbourhood meow.
When their bare feet racing to the end of the street
meet each other on the bottom step,
to tiptoe silently up, up, up, to the red doorstep.
When every light except ours is out.
When the pillows catch the last breath of twelve
and a silent yawn leads the way to a brand new day;
Midnight owls' flickering eyelids shut.

CHAOS

Through all of the chaos inside of me,
he said:
You simply make sense to me.

Every night, my heart
leapt out of my beating chest
into his gentle arms.
He gave this chaos rest.

ANXIETY

Pulsing.
Breath.
Overheating internally.
Chest pounding.
Ears ringing.
Hands shaking.
Nerves overtaking every bodily function.
Throat closes.
Salivary glands in overdrive.
Stomach shifts: thunderous storms
and fluttering wings.
Legs numb with anticipation of a
familiar face, unseen
for too many years to count.
Genuine excitement,
and yet,
inward,
only an animalistic, biologic, illogic
and entirely unnecessary
reflex to run as far and fast as possible.

Art: Marten Sealy

UNNECESSARY NOISE

You swear you're not usually like this,
so closed off and quiet,
always seemingly
having something to do.
You really don't.
Really, you're just here,
unclear of what to do
with your body and mind.
Whether to speak or listen to
an expanding silence you
used to LEAP into
and fill so far
it just became
noise
spilling out of you,
making little-to-no-sense
for the ones who
cared or dared to listen.

WHERE'S MY MIND

I've got
a
short span
of attention,

not to mention
the lack
of
direction

spinning me
consistently
where
my mind
longs to go.

Art: @stayawayfromblackhole

THE WAY I TEND TO BE

She said,
"So you're saying
I can say
absolutely anything under the sun
only to be heard by these four walls,
that door,
plus your two ears?
Never repeated or mistreated.
Not one syllable met with judgement
or critique,
for the entirety of my speech?"
"Correct."

She said,
"So you're saying
I can scream out,
dream out,
figure out what it is
that I want,
who I am,
why I am - the way I tend to be -
under the reflection of my own self-doubt?
Take up in arms and combat firsthand
what I let stand in my way,
with you guiding the way?"
"Correct."

She said,
"I think I'm ready."

"Great. We start today."

A FOOTSTEP AWAY

Red-knit shoulder,
leaning coldly on the rain covered window.
Cloth cap towards the incoming crowd,
looking down at your leather boots.
The brown strap of your watch
holding the ticking of time, too slowly.
I saw you instantly.
Toes tapping the water off of each other,
keeping themselves company
in the minutes before morning.

A footstep away,
my mouth opened to speak
but before I could squeak out
anything more than "Eek!",
you lit up, reached out,
the entire universe in your eyes,
and the smile on your face
before that embrace
forever holds a place in my heart,
that nothing will erase.

UNCONDITIONALLY

Unconditionally;
a one-sided eternity.
Six syllables
slipping out of those lips.
Once asked if said feelings
were unconditional,
for me - I confess: I wish it were yes.

I SEE YOU

It scared me
the way you held up that mirror
so blatantly.
The reflection, inescapable,
capable of so much sabotage.
Camouflaging my way through space
on a daily basis.
Inside, an oasis of disloyal faith
and hatred towards the unknown.

You flipped the mirror upside down.
My frown, now sweetly smiling at my feet.
A new feat, greeting her with empathy.
For once, with clarity.
A fraction of a second before my eyes weep while
remembering the used-to-be Decembers
I once put this person through.
Grateful for you
and all we've been through.
Today, I see someone new.

Art: Jada Powell

SUNDAYS WERE SIMPLE

Sundays were simple:
We'd wake up, disheveled,
mix up our feathered down duvet
around the room.
Sometime around noon:
Breakfast by the window,
legs crossed by the bedside table,
bacon and cinnamon
embedding into the carpet
of that apartment.
Evenings were eventful.
A tent full of memories,
christened for the holidays.
Grateful neighbours for our departure,
I'm sure.
Too much to squeeze into
that bachelor suite.
Somehow, two became one
and it worked.
Open the curtain,
you'd close it to be certain
no one saw our evening dances
through the doorways
of our 4-foot-kitchen days.
Frank and Ella, Louis, and Neil visited often,
and the occasional cookie deliverer.

How many hours you spent in that shower singing,
shy in the same room.
Your warmth in the morning,

before my eyes opened,
the sound of you almost closing the door
but then running and kissing me, half-asleep, "Just one more."
That room lives on in my mind.
A constant relapse of time,
conversations and late-night confessions.
We continue in circles, four corners
filling space in the place we used to call ours.

So much laughter and loving,
burning and crying.
Mostly on my part, that oven, appalling.
The milk cartons by the sink, still stink.
My hairpins still in stacks
in every crack of the carpet. Can't help it.
A lifetime with you still lives on in my mind.
Conversations repeating,
broken records still seeping
through the present,
taking me back to that room. Our home for a time.

Art: Jada Powell

SILVER SPOON

Fall.
Hard.
Face first in the dirt.
Wipe the mud on your sleeves,
past selves now desert.
Dig into the depths of the muck and disgust.
'Til the sun's light - ever so slightly -
hits the side of your eye.
Peripheral cry from your inner child.
Incessant shining, a mirror
flickering from a distance.
Dig.
Arms tired, resistance persists
and dismisses the reality of the world.
Surrounded by clay and dismay,
you find nothing more than
a small silver spoon.

Smudge the crud off
with the only clean corner of your shirt.
In the concave center:
find yourself.
See yourself.
Exactly as you are.
Completely covered in
everything you've uncovered from life thus far.
Start to slowly chip away at each bit with strife,
taking away only what serves, the rest silent to the
night.

It now hangs on my doorway.
Each time I step through,
I calmly remove any mud collected through the day
with my small silver spoon.

LAUGHTER LIES

When you're little,
it's all just a giggle.
The red eyes and smoke
pass through time,
no second looks.
But later,
as the years lag on,
the same shades in their glances
and smoke's daily dances
begin catching new nuances
between the cracks
of those familiar sounds.
The laughter changes tone -
becomes lonely.
Angry.
Sarcastic.
Drastically different
than what a little laughter ought to be.
And you realize it's been that way
the whole time.
Took me 23 years
to learn
that
laughter
sometimes
lies.

Art: Hannah Ockenden

UNPREPARED MONOLOGUE

Hi.
It's me - *laughs* -
who else would it be…
Just wanted to say "hi".
Hello. Hi.
Yeah. And ask how you're doing -
How are things? You doin' good?
Good.
Yeah.
Well.
I - uh. I've just… I've been -
Well, it's Christmas
and I've been thinking about you. A lot.
And hoping you're well.
Thinkin' of ya and sending my love.
Assume you're home for the holidays
with your family.
Sending my love to you all.
Call me if - yeah - if you want.
Talk soon then, yeah?
Hope you're well - already said that.
Yeah. Kay.
Bye.

Art: Aude Sawyer

LET GO

I've stopped
looking for you.
Marked what I want with what is true.
Removed the mask of
false pretenses
and inhaled in
the current circumstances:
You
let
go
so long ago.

Art: @fiorenza_art

WASTE OF TIME

There's
too much distrust
to discuss the fuss
you've mustered up
in the mess of my mind.
It would be
a waste of time.

FRIDAYS BELONG TO YOU

Lavender and fairy lights.
Oak Bay walks and pillow talks.
Mud streaks on your cheeks
and paisley pants loosely on your legs.
A sunset sprint and mid-day,
four-limbed starfish photo,
hung up in my personal hall of frames.
The smell of coffee in the morning,
honey bees on your knees.
A tightrope sling-shot, accompanied by
a handful - plus two - staples,
we can now laugh about.
Moroccan Bennies and Cinnamon Apple Cakes
always on two shared plates in that busy,
bustling box called The Blue Fox.
A sorcerer's staff in hand
and a snail on your nose.
Somewhere between
old soul and curious kid.
Smiling out at the bay.
On horseback.
Barefoot.
Shirt off.
Outback, on the lake,
summer swept out our feet.
The fondest of Fridays
belong to you, my frolicking friend.

Art: Forrest Shuster

ALONG THE WAY

Somewhere
along
the way,
we grew up.

Art: Jada Powell

N'EST-CE PAS

I have often heard or been told to:
"Treat people how you want to be treated."
But don't recall ever hearing the phrase:
"Treat yourself how you want others to treat you"
when both are of mutual importance.
N'est-ce pas?

Art: Mikaela Kruse

LOVELESS SILENCE

There's a limit to your love.
You'd fall asleep in my silence,
wrap me up in complaints of
your soft-spoken lies, hurt regrets and
tastes you placed too quickly on my tongue.
You spoke too quickly and out of turn.
Your love burned in places I know now are numb.
To this loveless silence we used to keep:

Goodnight, sweet dreams.
I hope you never wake from this peaceful sleep.

Art: Marten Sealy

MIND THE GAP

Stuck in a sardine can,
three million miles underground.
Feel like bursting out
some absurd mirage of humanity.
We're all yearning for it.
Toes tapping anxiously,
avoiding attempts
of glancing at each other -
When did eye contact become a crime?
Knees holding, fighting
to stay five metaphorical feet from our neighbours.
When did we become so fearful of one another?
Meant to connect.
Born curious.
Creatures giving and receiving
daily doses of emotions.

How do we do what we are meant to
while staring out into space?
Lined up faces, down the rows,
avoiding each other, nose to nose.
Feel like bursting out
some absurd mirage of humanity.
Don't you?

Art: Hannah Ockenden

VENOM

My venom stings,
it burns through skin
thick as three years
not over him.

CHEEKY

They say
she grins the ways in which
his limbs won't work.

Art: Hannah Ockenden

PHANTOM LIMBS

It doesn't matter which
side I sleep on,
I still feel you
on my skin.
Restless.
Rolling left,
then right.
Losing sight
of any amount of hours
that have ticked
by my bedside.
I've held you
nights like these.
I wish for one
still night, alone.

Normally,
my neck gets warm.
Then just under my ear,
when I feel your hands,
both sides of my thighs.
Nails tracing lines
along my spine's edge.
Ears hot.
Teeth bite
my lips.
They split.
Blood drips.
You lick.
Back's up.
You slip
between reality.
A tease, two years too long.

Art: @tara_rose_art

MORE THAN MEAT

Sometimes
the only thing
I see
is their eyes
all over me.

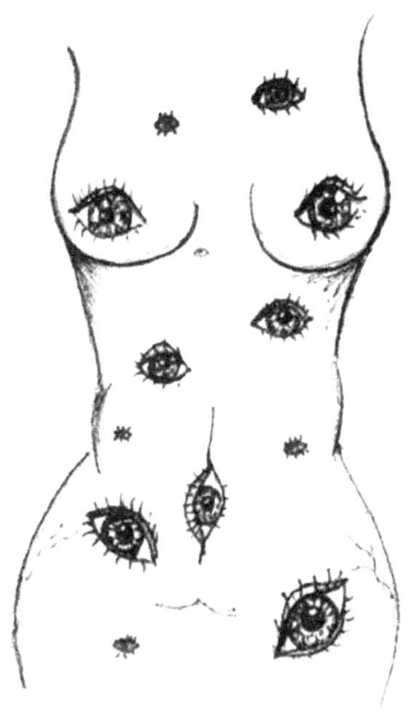

Art: Olive Elzinga

THE MOON WATCHED US FALL IN LOVE

The moon watched us fall in love.
She shone her spotlight across the waves
for our silver-lit slow dance
to the sound of crashing sea salt.
She lit the walk to the stars,
where we kissed and held the night close
to never let the moment pass.
She made sure to keep an eye on
the length between our sleepless nights,
laughing and falling into new mornings, again
and again and again.

She watched and spotlit
our little romance by the shores.
She lit the way for our little hearts
to hiccup and beat as our little feet
danced back and forth by Clover Point.
She sang us Neil Young and Van Morrison,
Elvis Presley and Louis Armstrong.
She drove our wheels across cities,
past lakes and rivers, over mountains,
through snow and rain and fallen leaves,
through trees and salty, slippery, shining shores.

The moon watched us fall in love
but I think she knows now,
when she glows,
that our feet dance out of sync.

Her eyes have closed
on our chapters of adventures
and she rains down light, in spite of the end.
She hears those songs
we no longer singalong to
and she inspires a new genre.

She watched our love come and go,
like the changing of tides
on Earth's every shore.
She mourns through sparkling tears,
though I know
she'll be standing by in the years to come,
shining down on new doors
and stories yet to surface.
She sees it all and through it all,
she glows, gifting us another night.

Art: Hannah Ockenden

READY WHEN YOU ARE

The 12 steps they do
take them to a dimension I want to meet.
Shake hands with and greet
with a tear and a cry
and a question of why I
have not thought of this before.
A friend I'd like to walk me down the aisle
of yesterday and tomorrow,
in pain and in sorrow.
The tear of growth and health
and discovering who's underneath
the skin I've been wearing,
constantly changing
since brought into this coloured world.
For addicts, perhaps,
but it's the realizations they grasp
that attracts my attention.
The dimension of depth they desire,
to depend on for undertaking
and shaking a new level of self.
That's where I want to go.
Ready when you are.

Art: Hannah Ockenden

NO ONE HAS EVER LOOKED AT ME THAT WAY

Third class of the day.
Too much caffeine having its way.
Bouncing basketballs of thoughts
in between every word you explained,
too slowly to follow.
Hands *ticking* and *tapping*.
Heels *clicking* and *clacking*.
"Come sit in a circle."
13 times 2
pupils staring back at you.
"Turn slowly.
See every set of eyes. Relax. Breathe."
Honestly, I can say I only noticed hers.
No one has ever looked at me that way.

The caffeine stopped beating.
My hands fell to the floor.
If I had a jaw, it ran out the door.
I didn't know whether I was standing or sitting,
or how many times the hand on the clock
went around, *ticking,*
before her eyes broke the small piece of eternity
I've always kept close to me.
Still, to this day,
no one has ever looked at me that way.

Her iris' colours danced onto the walls,
covering the room in waterfalls
of her greens and blues
and light grey hues.

We grinned simultaneously
and the warmth of her glowing smile
filled me from head to toe with desire
to move closer.
To hold her.
Rest her head on my shoulder.

Her eyes, fixing my body to the spot,
but my mind was afloat,
on a boat, between reality,
riding waves of her gaze,
electricity filling me.
It felt like she saw me, and I, her.
All of me. All of her.
Every bone's chiseled biology,
each other's psyche, and syncing heartbeats.
She flowed into my nerves
and I into hers.
Calming me with her gaze,
running through the maze
of this wonderfully infinite,
intimate minute.

The crowd noticed our moment.
Someone coughed nervously,
interrupting the silence suddenly,
cutting off our display of chemistry.
"Keep going"
I kept turning,
peering past others' eyes,
still skipping in her greenish-blue skies.
I didn't see anyone else but you that day.
No one has ever looked at me that way.

Art: Hannah Ockenden

BURNT GLASS AND NEEDLES

My mind's a cathedral of burnt glass and needles.
A fake throne, built of stone, so high it's illegal.
He's sitting there, grieving and teething and crying,
while bottles go flying and crashing and smashing
down to destroy all the walls built for this little boy.

If you don't believe me, ask her.
She deceived me.
Conceived it all up
as we laughed and you gawked
and the clock sort of stopped.
From then on, all you cared for
was her smiles and stares,
and countless, careless affairs.
And yet, here we are.
The boy's chair is falling far, and you don't seem to care.
You can't keep up with how quickly he's growing,
while you stumble and fall into all of the walls
you so carefully built with burnt glass and guilt.

She swallows and spits out the wine of safety,
blindfolds the boy and drives into the sun.
He is shaking and aching to be warm,
escaping all of the memories with toy guns.
He's waking from memories of
mum throwing bottles at daddy
and dodging the conflict.
He runs into the garden to digest the excess stress
he's exposed to and not yet supposed to ingest.
He's an infant for god's sake. Give it a rest.
But instead, she lays his head down

on a pile of burnt glass and tiles
she's had hidden in files her doctor's just opened.
You were asleep for so long.
She built castles so strong, now you're stuck
and a part of you will always be a stranger,
somewhere in danger.

So you pile up the bottles and burn them with diesel.
You pick up her antidepressant needles
and pile them higher and steeper until it eats her.
Until finally, she cracks and fills in the gaps
of the silent, confusing story
you've handwritten wrong.

The boy was a trap.

A gift, nicely wrapped,
to remind you of the mess you create
when you mate and digress to
the patterns and habits while
forgetting the ones you
have shined and shimmered at the crowds
and then limit to pockets you'll never revisit.

As I sit on my throne,
peering down at the piles,
and tiled aisles of your mistakes,
I hear him echoing your cries.
He's sitting, shaking, waiting to wake
and no longer anticipate
the crash of thunder over his head
with words that she and you said:
"I'll get them to fucking arrest you!"
9-1-1 can attest to
the unneeded furies in an infant's worries.
Memories that hold and mould

into his little head,
keep him from falling asleep in his bed.

5 years later,
he'll still remember the smell of your breath
and the hot hatred delivered.
5 years later,
he'll still get goosebumps
from shriveled up shivers of old slivers,
and past tense defense mechanisms,
and criticisms shouted over his head
from the woman who's finger
was locked and latched on, to wed.
You laid in her bed
while she worshipped another,
some younger stunner.

I sit on this throne and look down at the stones
built around this little boy,
"Come up to the top. Crawl through and don't stop.
There's a way and a reason for every strange season.
You'll be stronger than me and taller by at least 3
or 4 -maybe more- inches than the door.
Away from here. Away from this.
Away from nights of constant disarray and dismay.
I'm so sorry you're a product of dishonest construct.
Better not attest to the mess that she's made
as you grew and outgrew the test that she failed
as she flung you into this world
and surrounded you with fluffy blankets of fear.
I swear it's much better up here.
Climb through the needles
and bottles, guilt and shame.
Try as many as you need to along the way.
I'll wait. I realize it's in your DNA."

HOME

My toes are in the sand.
My face is in the sun.
All I hear is ocean waves.
My heart is full; I'm home.

Art: Megan Connors & Jasmine Annette

NATURALLY

He
was the only one
who ever really,
truly
knew me.
So naturally,
I ran
as far as the eye can see.

Art: Baran Ayguler

BLOOMING

I rarely recognize the girl in the mirror.
Come to see her reflection a little clearer.
Spot the freckles of
a six-year-old's summers
and the tiger's eye irises
gramma sang *Brown Eyed Girl* to.
Ah, so I do know you.
Though, I have not yet met
this particular
version of you until now.
How very lovely it is
to watch you grow,
and even though
- at times -
you know not
where you're going,
it's a pleasure just knowing,
your petals are blooming,
one day at a time.

Art: Hannah Ockenden

20 X SEVEN-YEAR-OLDS

I'm a shattering icicle of nerves,
a pool of melted ash,
in a room full of adults.
Four words make it out
then someone pours me a glass.

Now,
put me in a class
between twenty
seven-year-olds
and the possibilities are endless.
The hours are countless and
the conversation has no destination
but refuses to stop.
Tell me how that makes sense.

NEW HEIGHTS

Soul is stirring,
feeling
butterflies of change
approaching,
arranging space around
with wings and sound.
Swiftly lifting off
the ground.
New heights
in sight;
I'm so excited.

Art: Olivia Garstin-Collier

EXCEPTIONAL

She sat
and explained to me
the kind and colourful
world she sees,
and all I could
think was:

What an
exceptional
young woman,
sitting next to me.

Art: @fiorenza_art

WAITING FOR LIFE

Aren't we curious,
constantly holding onto
this concept of:

WAITING FOR LIFE

When it's already happening,
wrapping itself around us
every split second of the day.

But still, we say:
I can't wait
Until the day…
Until I have…
Until I go…
Until I am…
Until I know…

What on earth are we waiting for?

Art: Emma McEvoy

FAMILIAR FACE

"I remember you."
We met here,
last year- it was a disaster.
I thought I'd slipped past her.
She's persistent in being a part of my present.
A presence I once didn't welcome,
instead met with resent
and sent wallowing away
in cold corners, alone.
I'd like to think we've both grown.
"Come in, sit with me,"
Empathy said to Misery.

"Shh."

My sleepless thoughts
need some silence from
your shadow.
Let the light of the
night fill me up
and put me down
on my pillow next to
someone other than you.

SOMEONE NEW

Art: Jada Powell

UNQUESTIONED PRESCRIPTIONS

Seems strange that
the ones nowadays
responsible
for our health,
spoon-feed us drugs,
when the message
they conveyed
so clearly as kids was:

"Eat your greens and choose hugs!"

Steroids won't cure cancer.
Ritalin is not the answer.
Our minds, since birth,
are keepers and seekers of honesty.
Don't give them the key,
letting them lock up your mind,
confined to unquestioned
prescriptions on repeat:

"Here are your pills! See you next week."

Art: Hannah Ockenden

MAPLE SYRUP

It seems
A SIN
- if you believe in that sort of thing -
that something so sweet and satisfying
comes simply from a tree,
boiled and ready to be:
- Dessert
- Breakfast
- The top of all brunch
- A strange and very, very late lunch
- Nostalgic dinner
- Canadian headliner
- Guilt-free sweetener
- Sugar addicts' weakener
Syrup.
Spoon-feed me.

Art: Jada Powell

UNFOLDING

Sometimes,
things happen more smoothly
when you don't think so profusely.
When you let the pen hit the paper
and let the ink sink in and settle
to find what's in your mind.

Sometimes, it feels like
the thoughts that spill
aren't even mine.
Yet, I find them
unfolding in front of me,
one letter,
one line,
one full-length poem
at a time.

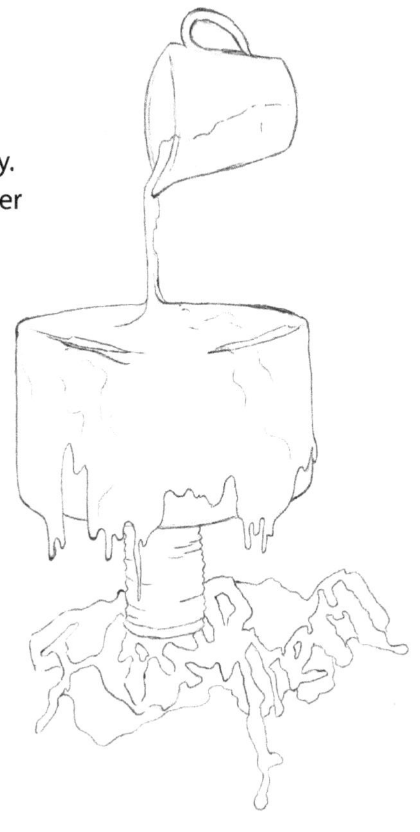

Art: Julie Mombourquette

SELF WORTH

I'm no saint but
I've learned to hold the weight
of how much more I deserve
than what I've ever settled for.

GEMINI

I'm a two-sided gemini.
A two-sided gem and I
would like to share the reason why:
I find it funny when you cry.
A tear spills over when you lie.
One side runs, the other hides.
Right side's loud but lefty's shy.

I often find the reason why is
my two-sided gemini.

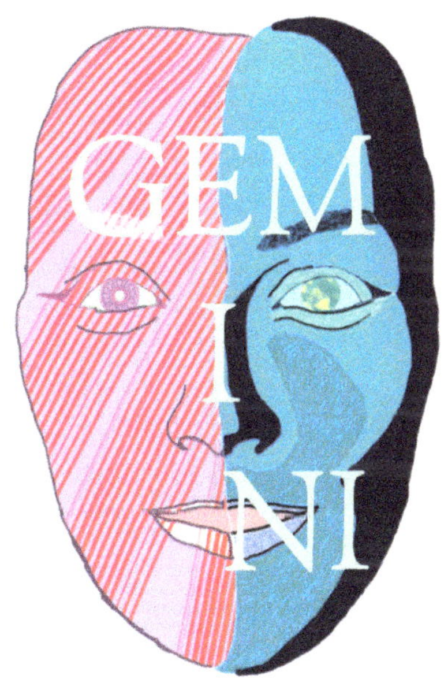

Art: Talia Woodland

SOARING

Saw a butterfly and named it after you.
Its wings brought summer
and sips of wine down my spine.
Its identical patterns
scattered thoughts of you
all over my spotless mind.
The rhythm of its beating wings had my smile
singing the songs of laughter you once sang so well.
The pace and space of your little silhouette,
spinning your way through the sky,
had little tips of tears
falling past my eyes.
You reminded my ears to listen for
the satisfying sound of someone
spreading their self-conscious wings
and flying so far beyond what anyone
could have anticipated.
Hope you're **soaring,**
just as high as I'd always predicted.
Today, you flew into my day as a butterfly
and my eyes caught yours
with only a smile.
I named it after you.

Art: Olivia Garstin-Collier & Alita

VOICELESS AFFIRMATION

I feel you in there
swimming,
almost brimming to the surface
of this inconsistent psyche.
I welcome you, take over,
unapologetically move over
the unnecessary chatter
and scattered words
telling me "I don't matter".
I refuse to give them power
over the voiceless affirmation that
I am in fact ENOUGH.

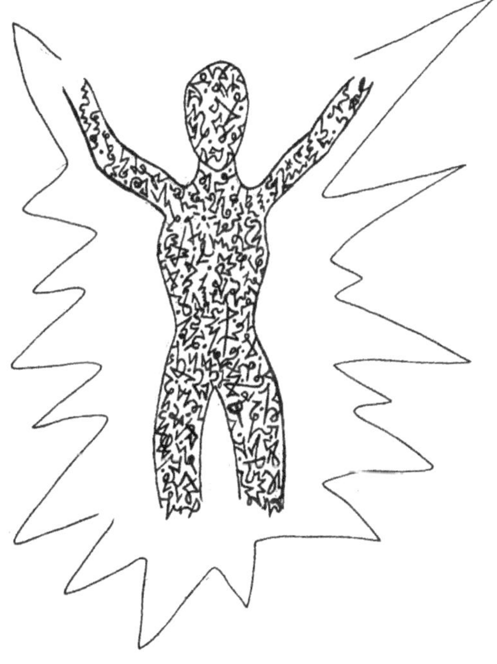

WHAT A DREAM

Did I ever tell you the story
of how our love freed me
from the fear of not
feeling for someone
what I dreamed falling in love felt like?

Art: @mariangela_artese

MAY I COME IN

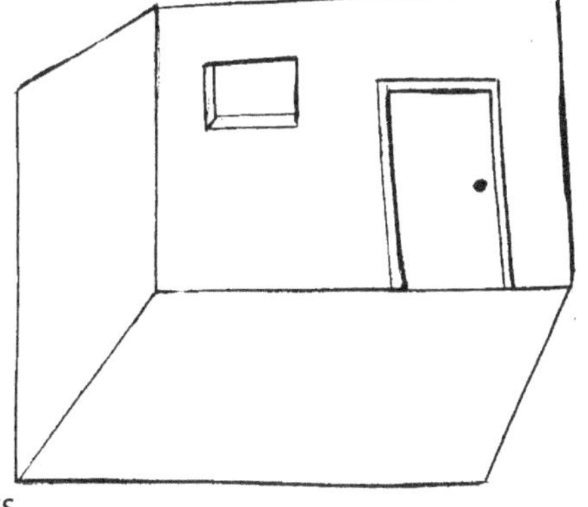

Every item
has a story
between four walls
and each sincerely intrigues me.
Infinite possibilities.
No one has the same
treasure chest as their neighbours.
I savour each of their scents, flavours,
their collections of stories
and personal memories.
Your room is my window into you.
An intimate collection you grew
with precision and distinction.

Each item placed; a deliberate decision.
An intimate realization of what you value.
Each framed face, choice of colour,
direction of the clothes hanging
one next to the other.
Each placed item;
A memory of you I'd like to meet,
shake hands with and greet,
take for coffee and a treat,
then dance with, in the street.

Your room is my door into your detailed interior,
the design of your incredible mind.
I notice, I do,
every detail,
- and if you

happen to be
anything like me -
each holds space for a thousand reasons,
but here are simply 3:

1. Value - held close by you
2. Requirement - proven necessary to you
3. Aesthetic - a visual pleasantry for you

We all find beauty and comfort differently
and surround ourselves accordingly.
For some it is simplicity.
Some, colour and variety.
Your four walls hold more stories
than you'll ever need
to sweep me off my feet.
I want to see how you define beauty.
Where to begin…
"May I come in?"

AN OCEAN FARTHER

The only eyes
I'll pursue
are of the brightest,
deepest blue;
after the depths you
brought me to,
I couldn't settle for
anything less than
an ocean farther
from where I've already been.

Art: Baran Ayguler

YOU WIN

I'm sending out the message.
Hope you get it.
If I write it,
I'll invite you to ignite it.
Flip the switch and pull
the pieces all apart
inside my heart.
These words belong to you.
Wish it weren't true.
But,
You.
It's you.
It's always you.
It's always been.
A thousand years 'n' still
it's you.
It's always you.
It's always been.
I lose, you win,
again.
I'm sending out the message.
Hope you get it.
If you see it,
please delete it.
Don't remind me.
Don't come find me.
Leave me hanging out the backside of your time.
Wish you were mine.
I'm fine.
I'm moving on.

Along.
Alone.
Looking for home,
without you.

I'll invite you
when I'm ready,
once I'm steady.
When these words stop spilling out,
filling pages I can't count.
Give me rest
until I dress
my wounds and woes.
God only knows -
If he exists -
how many minutes that consists of.
But for now,
this is the best that I can do:
1:00 am's thinking of you.
It's always you.
It's always been.
Call it a sin
because I've lost again.
You win.

DIAMONDS

Diamonds
on every surface area available.
In every colour,
every shape imaginable.
Fire engine red underneath,
swirling in on herself like a cinnamon bun.
The applause began.
The lights aglow.
The crowd screaming,
cheering for *HER* show.
The sound filling her shell, echoing into each layer,
louder than the last.
Slowly, she sneaks through the tunnel,
following the thunder to a spotlight on a stage.
They get louder as she peeks her cheek out from her shelter.
"ENCORE! ENCORE!"
She slips out further.
Whistles and shouts increasing,
reverberating through her cells.
Finally, a foot between her and safety,
when suddenly,
the storm stops entirely.
The crowd no longer cares.
Naked. Cold. Afraid.
She slinks back into her cave.
The lights fade.
Her diamonds turn to dust.

Art: Jada Powell

THE TASTE OF OUR FLAWS

I'd like to taste your flaws.
Embrace the rawness of your thoughts.
See through your days' unshown chaos.
A closet locked for onlookers outside of anyone but you.
Nothing but your truth.

I'd like to hold your flaws.
My hand in theirs.
Skip down the stairs onto the street
where sunlight shines so we can meet,
properly greet the day.
Set images down to lay
and stay until we're ready to confront them
and to question their intentions.

I'd like to laugh beside your flaws,
while exchanging shared assumptions
we've each had proven wrong
too many times to count
in exact, precise amounts.

I'd like to taste your flaws.
With freckled cheeks between my palms.
Lips meeting for the first time.
Their heart beating, knowing it's fine,
it's safe.
Its rhythm sharing music,
harmonizing with my too-quick
breathing, bashful heart.

Once worlds, now just a footstep apart.
Real.
Raw.
Open.
Scarred.
Not one ounce pretending
to be more than we are.

PUMPKIN PIE AND A MOONLIT SKY

No one smiles all the time.
Not even the moon.
Sometimes, her light shines softer
and certain freckles resurface
that haven't been out and about
for longer than a while
and the only ones who notice
are the nightly glancers,
the hopeless romancers,
catching it with their longing eyes.
Sometimes, the dimples on her cheeks
dance more daringly just before dawn breaks
and send her into the daily dream of waking up again.
Sometimes, the moon's eyes look sunken in and solemn,
to the point that one would almost swear
she'd just shed a tear or two.
But tonight, she smiles,
brightening a dark night with those
shy freckles and brave dimples
that only come out to *ooh* and *aah*
one little set of eyes, too small to spot:
The gal who's sitting, smiling back up at her,
somewhere on a park bench,
pinching bite-sized pieces of pumpkin pie to her lips,
while the other hand writes hopeful love letters to a smiling
moonlit sky.

Art: Julie Mombourquette

HOW CAN THAT BE

It bothers me that some
people find ease in
pronouncing and repeating
words like "rape" and "assault"
and "it's not your fault"
but when someone spills their story,
they fall speechless,
like the words sliced open
an uncomfortable silence.

How can that be?

You say it so plainly, mockingly,
between friends.
Making jokes,
"God, I'm glad that's not me."
But when somebody
tells you their story,
you turn the other way,
blindly.

How can that be?

Art: Hannah Ockenden

MORE MYSELF

I feel more myself
around you
than I do
in my own skin.

Art: Marten Sealy

AN OPEN BOOK

Well,
I can't stop
thinking about you,
and honestly,
I'd rather not hide.

Besides,
it wouldn't work if I tried.

See,
I wear my thoughts on my sleeves.
It's practically impossible
to deceive those around me
into perceiving
anything other than
precisely what I'm feeling.
Take a look: I'm an open book.

Art: Crystal Legoffe

READY OR NOT

To lie
is to dig yourself into debt.

Eventually,

you will payback,
whether you're ready or not.

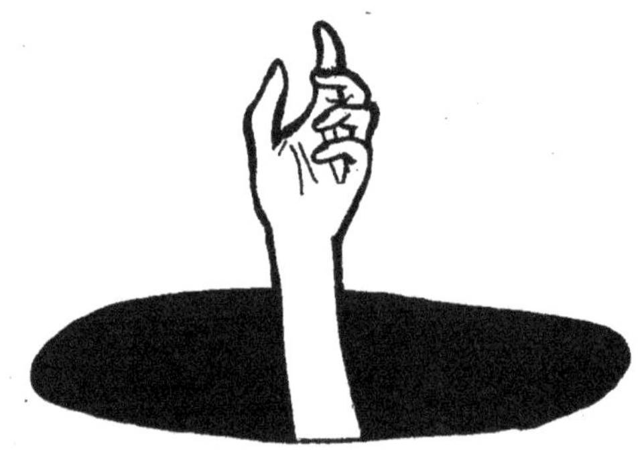

SALTWATER WHISPERS

She feels so far away.
Her constant waves,
a lullaby I barely remember the words to.
The rocking, hardly moving,
stilling in time apart.
My heart yearns to hear her songs,
run my fingers through her saltwater hair.
I pick up memoirs of her I've taken home,
place them gently on my cheek.
Instantly,
I feel my feet begin to sway.
I hear
whispers of her lulling laughter,
"I'm much closer than you think, my dear."

TOYING WITH MY THOUGHTS

They say we hold the key
to the control panel of our own mind,
but a part of me feels like
you stole it from me
and have been taking great pleasure
in the drawn-out, drastic amount of time
that you've been toying with my thoughts on rewind.

Art: Hannah Ockenden

TWO FOOLS

Goodnight
love and heartbeats
followed by fluttering wings
and gazes for hours
at you,
at stars.
Look at us two fools
swinging our feet in cold water.

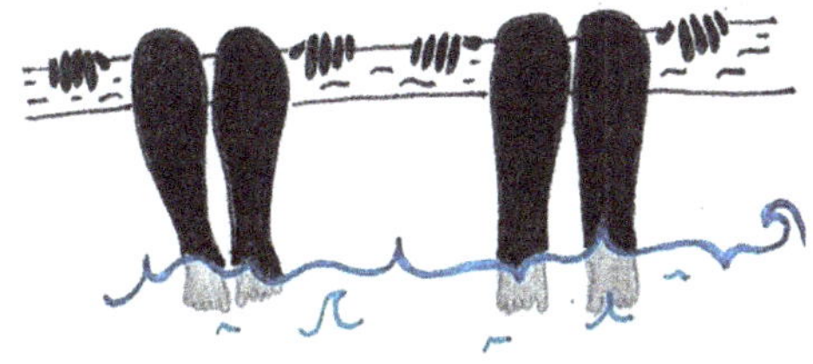

Art: Jada Powell

EVOLVING MACHINES

We're all evolving into machines
that speak words and project screens.
You are what you eat,
and when all you do is look down at your feet,
nothing will meet you at eye level
and speak to you at the level you seek.

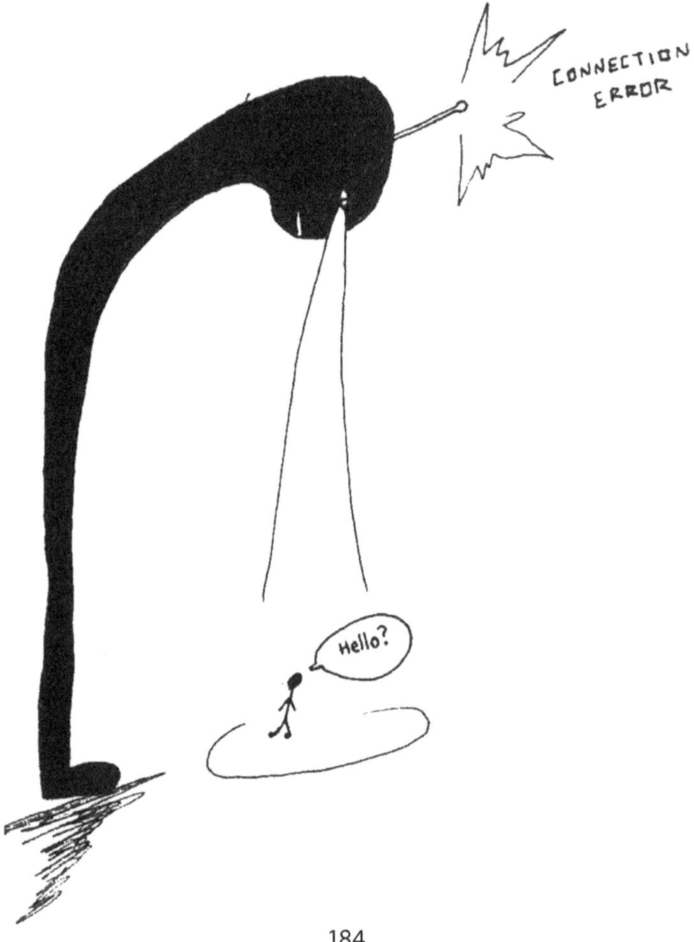

THANKS FOR LISTENING

Trapped.
Snapped.
Lost track of the stacking up
stock of emotions, locked in,
unavailable to onlookers,
stuck inside one skull.
Always pushing the inability
to hold onto more imaginary weight
than what equates to
an equal, balanced state.
What to expect from
neglecting any form of self-reflecting?
"I'm fine"
too many times
turns into a snapped line.
We are more fragile than inclined to admit.
Nonetheless, it's a bitch.

Filled.
Spilled.
Leaning out the window sill,
gasping for air.
Full of words I wouldn't dare
verbally share -
until you.

Thank you
for conditioning my mind to unlock
the box of overflowing thoughts -
as you do -
and once again,
bringing peace in release.
"Better out than in."
Thanks for listening.

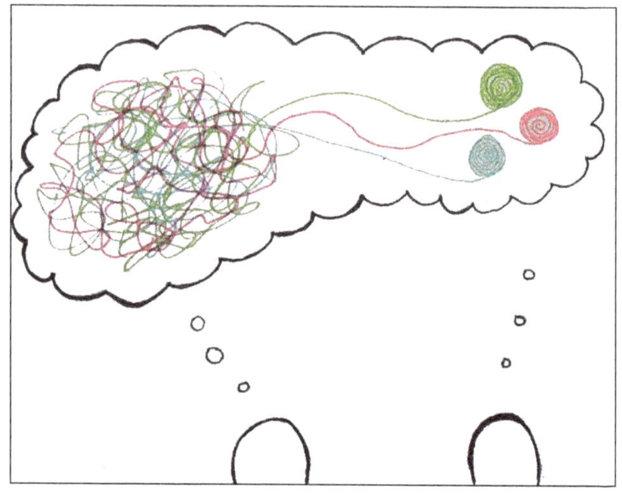

THE SMELL OF SPRING

In spring,
we skip along
the cherry blossom trees
lined up, abundantly blooming,
sharing bashful snowflakes
that fly above our heads,
gently float to coat the streets
in a sea of pink,
and dance between our feet.
We drive past our favourite trees
every sun-shiny morning
to greet the day with
a smiling inhale
of the only scent I've ever dreamt of.

ACROSS GALAXIES

Constantly chasing
hidden treasures,
chances beyond measure:

the possibility of two entities
stripping each other blind
and sending their love
across galaxies.

Art: Hannah Ockenden

SMALL TALK

Ask me about the weather **one more time**
and I'll stick my foot in your mouth
and ask you when the last time you had a **real** conversation
was.

Talk to me about:
The last time you laughed so hard your belly ached.
A habit you want to break.
The best meal you ever ate.
Who makes you feel the most comfortable.
Tell me about your childhood, or what makes you feel
vulnerable.
If you had kids, what you would name them.
Show me the constellations you know and how to find them.
Recount your favourite day thus far in life.
What your relationship with your dad is like.
How you manage life's stressors.
The crush you had on a past professor.
What you think about aliens and galaxies.
Your pet peeves and insecurities.
Something you've always wanted to do.
What drives your roommates crazy about you.
The weirdest sex you ever had.
The best sex you ever had.
Sing me your favourite lyrics.
Share the reason you were last in hysterics.
Who's in your head at night.
If you believe in afterlife.
Someone you miss.
Your first kiss.

Tell me a new year's resolution you haven't gotten to yet.
A joke you'll never forget.
What you would do if you won the lottery.
A strange favourite hobby.
A lie you wish you could take back.
The composer of choice for your life's soundtrack.
An apology you've been wanting to deliver.
An emotional trigger.
Your favourite smells
and if you believe in magic spells.

There are **infinite possibilities**
of which direction a conversation could go.
So don't tell me about the cloud.
I don't care and neither do you.
Tell me something you actually want to.

FIRE AND FLAME

I feel so far away.

The glaze over their realities.
Reaching through fog incessantly.
Feel irritated,
weighted,
Restless.
Distressed by the thought that
they're unsatisfied with their lives
enough to cover every detail
and subtlety in fire and flame.
Smoke and drain out
any mundane, humane
feeling from their daily existence.
Running through the rain
of their insincere
parades of entertainment,
which always arrive unnaturally.
6 times a day, specifically:
Before dinner.
After dinner.
Before bed.
Upon waking.
Before lunch.
After lunch,
and so on, so forth,
days in, days out.
Another red night.
Another red day.

They feel so far away.

Art: Hannah Ockenden

OUR HOME IS HER MUSEUM

Brush our teeth over a blue sink.
Bathe in rainbow waters.
Exit next to Klimt and his painted daughters.
Tiptoeing over Iranian rugs.
Sipping out of Ukrainian mugs.
Walk down halls of summer sun rays.
Lapis butterflies on custard walls
coated in reds and lavender
upon becoming a teenager.
Take plates from orange creamsicle coloured cupboards.
Fall asleep counting glow in the dark stars
and moons on purple sarongs covered in crescents.
Tie-dyed socks scattered over the floor.
Drawings, collages, paintings
and sculptures starting from the frame of the door.
A mirror's reflection of a thousand colours
in every direction.
A wardrobe organized in the colours of the rainbow,
each with at least 3 shades of the same flavour.
Matching tablecloths with napkins.
Paisley, mandala and floral bedding.
Worldly collections.
Masks from continents I've not yet seen.
Photographs framed, standing forever still
in distant places we've been.
Hand-painted vases, bottles, bowls,
cups, plates, jewels, gems,
and an enormous plastic engagement ring
from her days of bartending.
Our home is her museum.
A display of her fondest, coloured memories.

EVER AFTER

The story is never
"Happily ever after."
The End. Finished. Finito.
No.
Just because you've found another
doesn't stop the story altogether.
The pages thereafter
are of the most valuable treasure.
We leave out the most important part,
expecting everyone's story's end to start
to be cookie-cutter classic:
Fairytale plastic.
"It's romantic."
Oh, please.
Yes, down on his knee is
a gentleman's classic
that will come, then continue
with trials and trips you
were never expecting.
Just because the wedding
is over and done with
doesn't mean
the book's cut off clean.
The journey together
through the stormiest weather
will determine whether
you'll truly remain a pair,
happily, for "ever".

BOA

I cannot wait to meet you, greet you,
hold you in my arms, and squeeze
your little baby feet.
A minute ago,
we were babies too,
now, here comes you:
A fresh beginning,
somehow spinning up
our space and time.

Let's rewind
and hold this minute
just a thousand seconds more.
I simply adore
- before the moment you were born -
every piece and part of you.
And soon you will see the reason,
when you feel, inside,
the love that shines within.

Art: Hannah Ockenden

CHOREOGRAPHED SISTERS

Running around and around,
cutting corners of the carpet,
rounding rectangle - edges.
Bouncing contently
through the musical medleys.
Diamonds on the Soles of Her Shoes
playing all through
the soundtrack of their childhood.
They'd miss the beat,
step early or too slowly,
fall down, spin around
and skip the other way, singing,
day by day.
Until
they outgrew the carpet -
now the length from their head to their toes -
music playing that no one else knows,
their four feet moving simultaneously.
Each beat, perfectly timed and predicted.
Choreographed sisters,
shifting side to side,
laughing.
Chasing movement.
Collective students.
Teaching each other each step of the way,
day by day.

Art: Hannah Ockenden

IN THESE PAGES

Each time we meet
two sets of feet's new phases,
my mind whispers:
Will he be the one who stays?
All the others end up in these pages.

FOREVER MY STARS

I hear whispers of four sisters
giggling, skipping down Italian streets,
sipping down pink champagne.
A reckless decision,
quickly forgiven:
Four stars engraved.
Four stars remain.
Pieces of each other,
memories -
hidden or displayed,
depending on the day -
forever on our skin.
Near or far,
forever my stars.

Art: Dania Soum

THE ONES WHO WERE WILLING

I share a lot of

surface substance,
contained conversation,
filtered thoughts
and liquid laughter,
hyper outbursts
of energetic aesthetic,
empathetic hours of hearing others' hurts.

Easily.
Everywhere.
Effortlessly.

Until I'm
safely
somewhere,
unquestionably cared for,

I share very little

unmasked emotion,
raw thoughts and
genuine notions,
past breaks
and current hopes.

It takes time for my arms
to feel the embrace
you're willing to share.

It takes months for my lips
to trust the taste of honesty.
Takes years for my ears
to believe every inch of you
undoubtedly cares.

So, to the ones who were willing
to withstand the wait.
For the ones who stayed,
stuck around to uncover the true shades.
To the ones who've seen every colour
kept quietly at bay,
and who still remain close, to this day:

Thank you,
for giving me your hand and dancing daringly into a genuine
truth.

REALITY CHECK

IN MOVIES:

The girl falls for the only-slightly-older-than-her,
dashingly gorgeous professor,
who is a little too hard on her
or simply ignores her in class for the first half.
Ever notice in movies, dance studios always have
4-story wooden ceilings with skylights,
and windows overlooking
the only bits of nature in big cities- beside the point.
After months of swallowing down her courage,
trailing in his footsteps,
she finally builds up the audacity
to burst through the gigantic fairytale studio doors,
wearing the flowy, flattering dress that ties at the back.
All hair down "naturally"
that somehow never gets in her face
as she boldly interrupts his in-session dance class
and belts out
"I'm in love with you!"
and leaps into his tanned, toned arms.
He catches her effortlessly and caresses her as he says it back,
and they dance for an entire song
looking longingly into each other's eyes. Credits roll.
Lalala. Fluffy fluff. Woah.

IN REALITY:

The girl invites her best friend's brother over -
whom she has had a crush on since her very first sleepover -
to her 4-bedroom apartment that smells like
3 different kinds of incense and Britney Spears' CIRCUS
perfume.
"Tonight worked out great, right?"
Her roommates all have boyfriends
and are out for double date night.
Except for Genevieve, who's off in France indefinitely,
chasing her ex-alcoholic muse - beside the point.
She prepares the only Italian cuisine she knows,
from the cookbook she got for Christmas when she was 13
years old.
Half a bottle of cheap wine down, sweating.
Half laughing at everything he says.
She manages to look into his eyes for longer than a second
and awkwardly squawks,
"I think I love you - ohhh wha -"
Covers her mouth quickly.
He chokes on his spaghetti.
Coughs it back up onto his plate,
(what not to do on a fifth date)
and recovers, laughing out, "Are you kidding?"
Judging by the unfortunate look on her face,
he swallows a resurfaced piece of
half-chewed, overcooked pasta,
wipes the store-bought sauce off of his face,
mentally prepares and painfully replies,
"I'm sorry. I'm just not ready. Thanks for the macaroni."
He gets up apologetically and leaves early.

MORE OFTEN THAN NOT

My mind wanders and ponders
- more often than not -
over whether he's reading
or what he's thinking
while repeating these words in his mind.
Does he know which lines are strictly mine
and which belong to his memory,
wrapped in his laughter
and English banter?

My mind wanders and ponders
- more often than not -
over whether
he searches for himself
between these tinted,
forever printed lines.
If the signs and symbols
spell out his name
as clearly as they do for me.

So, dear reader,
if you currently find yourself
holding a book of our memories,
I'll take this opportunity to
thank you, irrevocably.

STILL DANCING

Most people run indoors.
"Out of the rain!"
Cover their heads.
Skip over puddles.
Too cold, too grey.
Hide inside. Stay away.
Say I'm insane.
Sound of consistent showers on the roof:
Sprinting out of the room,
morning, night or afternoon.
Door flung open.
3 layers soaked-in.
Rainwater
all over my skin.
"Is she *still* dancing?"
Of course! Are you kidding?

GOODNIGHT MR. SUN

Sun strokes my skin
and I feel the breath of summer
slowly fading south.
Leaves licking my feet,
leaving their little nooks on less alive branches.
Wind whispers up my arms,
goosebumps, jumping jacks around the cracks in the roads.
Changing breeze, I sneeze and cuddle the blanket closer.
The sky is clear but winter is near.
Here and there we run to catch
the last snatch of summer's sweet songs.

Goodnight Summer Sun.
Sweet dreams along your wait
behind the big boulders and bridges of mountain ridges.
I'll see you again my friend,
and until then, I await my new fate, flickering in the frost.
I look forward to seeing you again,
so we can catch up on all that's happened up until then.

It felt so - well there's no word for it -
to finally get it out of my system.

The relief from releasing the grief,
being held and told I was worthy of love.
That it wasn't my fault.
That I had nothing to be ashamed of.
Sitting in a room full of strangers who held my hand
and made every immediate change possible to my
circumstance
for me to feel any kind of justice, comfort and empowerment.

This is not normal behaviour.
This should **never** be "NORMALIZED" behaviour.
No one should be used to
hearing about it/talking about it.
No one should be desensitized to it.

Those words should not slip out so easily.
So apathetically cold. Careless.

A crime with no cuffs, no case,
no proof or prosecution
does not mean that it did not happen.

So,
to any who choose to
or refuse to
fight silently:

I respect you.
I support you.
I believe you.

#METOO

"GOOD LOOKS"

You try growing hair
involuntarily everywhere
and instantly being told
to rip out every follicle,
before the age of twelve.
It's simply unnerving.
Serving no purpose
other than "good looks".
Before they're even microscopic
you've learned:
shaving,
waxing,
chemically infused creams,
plucking/tweezing,
sugaring,
lasering,
process of electrolysis,
bleaching,
threading,
epilating
FOR
full body, limbs only, bikini, Brazilian,
upper lip, chin, cheeks, nose, brow bone -
Have I made my point?
It's too much to appoint a pre-teen
- or any human being, for that matter.
Twelve years old, already fearing
showing femininity at work.
Quite frankly, it's berzerk.

Art: Jada Powell

HUMANITY

Know what's sad?
How much we know
and still refuse to grow.

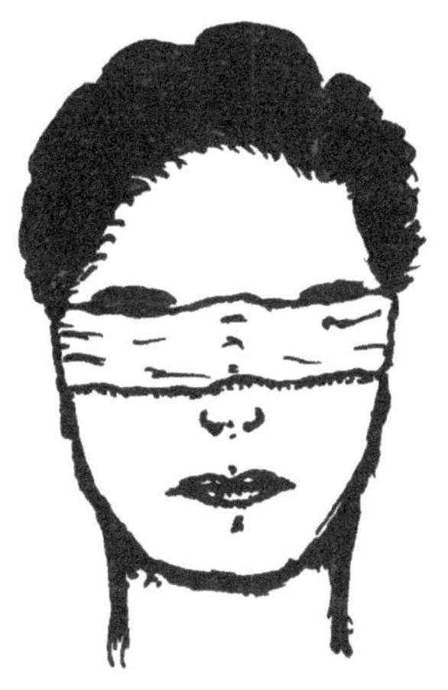

Art: Hannah Ockenden

WALKING THOUGHTS

"You don't suppose there may be
a greater purpose at stake?

And that perhaps
we're all part of a greater fate than
that which we envision
and embark on daily,
in our adventurous,
seemingly aimless meandering?

There's just so much more
going on
than what any of us
truly have all of the answers for.

After all,
*we **are** infinite.*
What do you think?"

Art: Lonnie Powell

TEARS> ANGER

Don't cover me
with your tempered umbrella.

I never asked.

In fact,
I much prefer the rain.

Art: Jada Powell

ALMOST

I think I'm finally on the brink
of thinking of your face.
Of wandering through
the world of memories we made.

I think I've almost reached the point
of moving past your mind
and becoming un-entwined
in the mess we made.

Art: Hannah Ockenden

Someone else's kiss…
My lipstick shouldn't taste like this.

SOMETHING IS AMISS

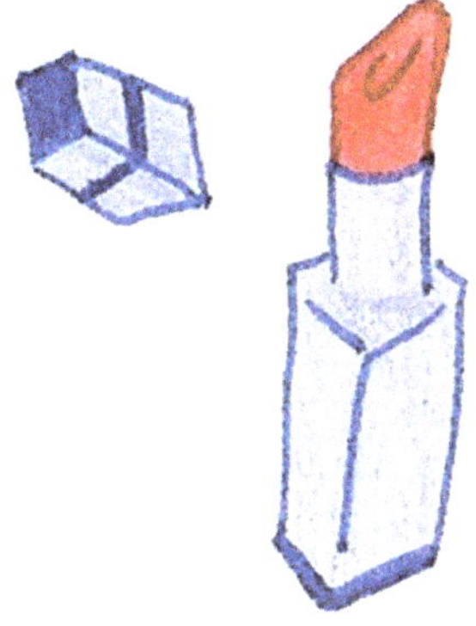

Art: Jada Powell

DO-IT-YOURSELF

Poetry
and naked kitchen dances

=

Easy D.I.Y. home remedies for self-diagnosed A.D.D.

Art: Jada Powell

SIMPLY AND COMPLETELY FEELING

I had a dance teacher who used to say she
LOVED emotions.
Extreme highs, lows,
ins, outs,
ups, downs,
all arounds-
you name it: she loved it.
She used to say
she would allow them to fill her,
head to toe,
feel it pour through her bones.
Whatever emotion it was that day
would do or say
everything and anything
that lead the way in its shoes-
you should have seen her dance.
She used to tell us to embrace our emotions
because they're each a full-body reminder that we are **ALIVE**.
She explained the beauty
in our ability to **FEEL**
so many indescribable possibilities,
and for it to constantly be shifting,
even in a short period of time.

She used to say
the euphoric wave would ebb and peak,
then eventually,
and inevitably,
slowly flow and leave a fading glow
of a calm silence between.
She felt clean.

Fresh.
Rejuvenated.
Like her pores breathed in new fresh air
and the view changed landscapes,
standing still.

Imagine that.
How incredibly, insanely simple:
To feel every inch of our humanity,
unapologetically.
To wrap ourselves in our emotions.
Fill our lungs and torsos with devotion,
our hips, hands and knees with joy,
our fingertips with anger
and our tongue with empathy.
Every limb to find the edge of
each end of humans' emotional spectrum.
Our ears to feel tears,
noses to tickle with disappointment,
our pinky toes to trip and fall over boredom
and our sternums to burn with jealousy.
How terrifying.
How beautiful.
Each body part
a piece of art,
breathing life, in all its glory.
Shocking honesty.
Is it strange that this is my fantasy?
An exhibition of humanity.
Unmasked.
Unfiltered.
Uncovered.
Uncut.
Unveiled.
Simply and completely
FEELING.

LACE AND COTTON

Only two women have struck my lungs,
caught me off guard,
held my feet above ground.
Sent me spinning standing still.
I remember them well:

1. Short, sun-kissed brown hair.
Green eyes and mystery.
No hint of history.
Just suddenly dropped into my lap,
quite literally.
Grey dress covered thighs
alongside my dancing hands.
Eyes closed.
Muffled voices.
Too many to count, muted out.
She smelled like vanilla sundaes
and tasted like surprise.

2. Auburn hair.
Stared right between my lies.
Eyes flirting without words.
Heartbeat stirred.

Ease in intimacy with everybody,
one by one until she reached me.
Her hands dancing over skin
without hesitation or sin.
Simple intricacies:
lace and cotton,
long sleeve, unbuttoned.
Speaking tongues.
Laughing lungs,
strung out on the walls.
Hiding our held hands down the halls.

Art: Hannah Ockenden

WITHOUT THE MASK

For years
I feared that
without the mask,
the simple task of
luring them in
would shew them off.
Push away
any say
in whether my blank face
would create
the same compassion
and interest
in peoples' reactions.

I feared
without the extravert colours
and the smiling cheekbones,
without the dimples
and energized eyes,
that no one would
care to hear my voice.
Instead, they'd deny
the truth
over a myth.

Convinced my mind:
without a mask,
I was unwanted.
An empty canvas to the crowds.

But,
through shedding
23 layers of
paper maché mirrors,
piece by fragile piece,
I've made peace
in learning that
showing underneath
is weakness at its peak:
The strength that I seek.

FANCY

It is said
that we are drawn to
people we are subconsciously
physically attracted to.

So-
in a sense-
your friends all fancy you.

Just some food for thought.
You're welcome.

DEPTH OF SUNSHINE

I'm incredibly attracted to her colours.
The worlds she paints with her words.
The light between her thoughts
and sprinkles of her laughter.

I'm in awe of
how she embraces shadows
like they're kin.
The kindness she brings in.
The dept of sunshine within.

Art: Hannah Ockenden

COLLEGE IS LIKE…

Fumbling through your tickle trunk,
trying on every outfit in it
then walking out wearing it.
Parading the colours
and meeting the mirrors
that reflect back anything outside
of the four walls you've stared at your whole childhood.

Continuously.

Until you find
the fit that feels
most like you:
the most comfortable truth.
Then, sharing it with the world,
unapologetically.

Art: Hannah Ockenden

Sitting in past dreams come to light.
Still somehow covered in long lingered sights
and frights of yesterdays, long ago.
Where are you **now**?
What do you want **today**?
This moment to the next.
Why knot yourself and plot your past into your present,
when it's long gone and drawn on too long?

MOVE ALONG

Art: Jordy Locke

FLATTERY

If you want to shower me in flattery,
show me yourself, honestly.

VANILLA ICING

She took my hand and lept,
who knows how many hundred feet,
into a pool of darkness.

I'm shaken to the sunlit surface,
awakened by the softness
of her silver hair
dancing around my head,
tickling my cheeks.

Ears engulfed in turquoise ripples.
Floating on our backs.
The crown of our heads
resting on each other's right shoulders.
Mirror image of light and dark
spinning in pools of water.

I don't know how long we laid there,
breathing,
grinning,
spinning in circles.
Waterfalls landing
like vanilla icing
over our shoulders.

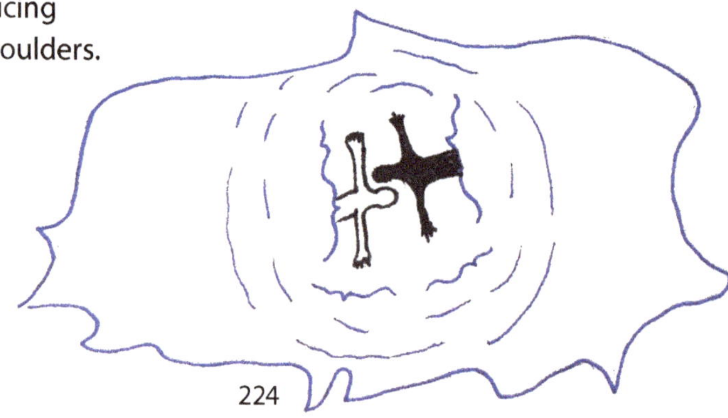

I NAMED HER LADY

She picked me up
when no one could find me.
Lost in my mind,
spaced-out in time.

Each of her strings
hugged words back into me.
Lungs full of life
after months on end
of chaotic silence.

The warmth of her sound
wrapped me in
a bouquet of flowers.
A cocoon of petals,
helping my wings
bloom again.

She brought music
to my ears,
to my arms,
shaking through every atom,
feeling more than words.
When I picked,
her sounds filled me,
pouring joy through every limb.

Suddenly obsessed with her laughter.
Excited for each new day,
to meet her again

and reach a new feat together,
smiling with a friend.
The music, giggling out of her belly,
tickling my fingertips
as she taught me to play.

The universe laughs in flowers
and she was mine,
picked out of a quaint music shop.
My little sunshine.
I named her Lady, like the bug.
Some say they're lucky- I think they're fun.
Go out and find yourself one.

STRANGER

People see what they want to see,
and usually
it's a version of me I'd like to meet.
Who is she?

PERSONAL POSSIBILITIES

It's too much pressure
to remain
one type of person
for an entire existence.

Surely flowers don't
suddenly
bloom into butterflies,

but reinventing
your personal possibilities
is never "not an option".

Art: Jenn Kehoe

★ ILLUSTRATORS ★

1. Hannah Ockenden
2. Jada Powell
3. Baran Ayguler
4. Lonnie Powell
5. Marten Sealy
6. Dania Soum
7. Jenny Hawes
8. Forrest Shuster
9. Megan Connors
10. Jasmine Annette
11. Jenn Kehoe
12. Talia Woodland
13. Julie Mombourquette
14. Jordy Locke
15. Karly Fredrickson
16. Maisie Rose
17. Mikaela Kruse
18. Emma McEvoy
19. Sidney Cummings
20. Olive Elzinga
21. Aude Sawyer
22. Jo Barnes
23. Olivia Garstin-Collier
24. Crystal Legoffe

Instagram Artists

@hannah.boshana
25. @mariangela_artese
26. @poetryncolor
27. @broken_isnt_bad
28. @_danijelaa__
29. @sidraws_
30. @fiorediop
31. @ma_goa
32. @notart.jpeg
33. @lilla.clara
34. @wi_kaminska
35. @laurenmaria.b
36. @hello_hann_
37. @oh_long_leslie
38. @_augustobm
39. @tara_06
40. @stayawayfromblackhole
41. @pride_nyasha
42. @fiorenza_art
43. @kingasarts
44. @tara_rose_art

★ ABOUT THE AUTHOR ★

Alita Lee Andrea Powell is a
24-year-old Canadian, from
Whitehorse, Yukon. She is a
goofy and energetic performer,
traveler, TEFL teacher, and ocean
enthusiast. Alita graduated
from the Canadian College of
Performing Arts and recently
returned from two years in Italy
and Spain, teaching English
through theatre.

When Alita's not working, she is most likely writing, dancing,
playing the ukulele, eating chocolate with her sister and
brother-in-law, or imitating worldly accents.
Find more of her poetry on Instagram: @l.i.l.luna

CPSIA information can be obtained
at www.ICGtesting.com
Printed in the USA
LVHW070716120820
662929LV00044B/1107